San Angeleños

San Angeleños

MEXICAN AMERICANS IN SAN ANGELO, TEXAS

by Arnoldo De León

Department of History, Angelo State University

66948

Fort Concho Museum Press
213 East Avenue D
San Angelo, Texas   76903

Book designed by Gus Clemens
Maps drawn by Miki Ross Clemens

ISBN 0-938036-05-X

Published for Fort Concho Museum Press by
Mulberry Avenue Books
2609 A&M Circle, San Angelo, Texas 76904

Printed in the United States of America
by Newsfoto Yearbooks, San Angelo, Texas

First printing, January, 1985

para mis padres

Jesús y Julia De León

TABLE OF CONTENTS

NOTE ON USAGE

Words of Spanish origin which are part of common English usage and found in English dictionaries are not italicized and are not defined in the text.

Spanish words which are commonly used by the subjects of this book but which are not part of common English usage are *italicized* and defined only on first use.

The terms Hispanic, Mexican, Mexican American, and San Angeleño, are used according to the following definitions:

Hispanic: Anyone with cultural origins in a Spanish-speaking country; often identified by a Spanish surname. Includes Mexicans, Mexican Americans, South and Central Americans, Puerto Ricans, Cubans, and others.

Mexican: A citizen of Mexico.

Mexican American: Any inhabitant of the United States who has Mexican cultural origins.

San Angeleños: Hispanic residents of San Angelo.

Preface

These pages contain the history of Mexican Americans in San Angelo, a city of 73,240 inhabitants located at the confluence of the North, Middle, and South Concho rivers—the "Concho Country" of West Texas. In 1980, Mexican Americans comprised twenty-three per cent of the population of the city, approximately the same percentage as Mexican Americans in Texas as a whole.

As the number, power, and influence of Mexican Americans continues to increase in Texas, it is important to reflect upon the history of Hispanics to give perspective to the present and insight into the future. Although this book will be of particular interest to people of the Concho Country, it should have significance throughout the Southwest to those interested in Mexican American history.

Several themes run through the narrative which unfolds. Change is the most obvious; communities are seldom static. During the past twelve decades the Mexican American community has changed both within itself and in its relationship with the larger San Angelo community. This book chronicles and examines those changes.

Assertiveness in bringing change about is a second theme of the Mexican American presence in San

Angelo. Through the years, Mexican Americans have employed different tactics to prod things their way, sometimes with minor effects, sometimes with great success. The significant thing is that Mexican Americans sought to define their own destiny. This was evident in San Angelo's beginning, and the tradition was maintained by the LULAC, the G.I. Forum, delegations of individuals, and elected officials.

Ethnicity and cultural continuity is another theme. The term Mexican American has been an appropriate label from 1867 to the present. Of course, there always have been some Mexican Americans who are thoroughly assimilated into Anglo society and may even shun ethnic labeling. But historically, San Angeleños (a term I use throughout the book as a name for Mexican Americans of San Angelo) have remained faithful to their Mexican background and acknowledge it proudly. Despite commitment to American institutions and belief in what the United States represents, most have preferred to retain elements of their cultural past.

At least two things have urged me to write about Mexican Americans in San Angelo. First, no local history heretofore has focused on Mexican Americans. This is true even though Mexican Americans have been a part of San Angelo since it sprouted across the river from Fort Concho. This book is thus an effort to rectify the gap in the historical record. My second reason for writing about San Angelo was personal—my interest in past events naturally led me to probe the story of a community in which I live.

Numerous individuals contributed toward the completion of this book. Those who permitted me their time so that I might profit from their recollections of San Angelo history deserve my foremost thanks. Their names are listed in the bibliography. Mario J. Cruz, Oscar C. Gómez, and Al Celaya read portions of the manuscript and added valuable commentaries, primarily for chapters 4 through 8. Most valuable in the same respect was a lengthy and frank critique by the distinguished attorney Ed Idar Jr., now retired in

Austin, Texas, which forced me to clarify my understanding of recent times.

As usual, my sincere thanks go to Professor Malcolm D. McLean of the University of Texas at Arlington, who has acted as the most vociferous critic of my written works since I completed my graduate training. He edited this work with usual efficiency.

I also thank Wayne Daniel, Fort Concho librarian/archivist, who saw virtue in the work and solicited it for Fort Concho Museum Press; John Vaughan, Fort Concho director, who sees Fort Concho Museum Press publications as one of Fort Concho's responsibilities to the San Angelo community; the Fort Concho Museum Board, which gave the study its staunchest backing; and Gus Clemens, project editor of the Fort Concho Museum Press, who gave the manuscript its final editorial touch.

CHAPTER ONE

Spanish Activity and Mexican Arrivals, 1541-1880

Less than fifty years after Columbus discovered America and only twenty-two years after the first sighting of the Texas coast by Alonso Álvarez de Piñeda, the planting of Hispanic roots in the Concho Country began. The first to come was Francisco Vásquez de Coronado, the "Golden Conquistador," who had been looking in New Mexico for cities of gold and turquoise. When Pueblo Indians persuaded him to search to the east in 1541, Coronado and an army of more than a thousand men marched onto the Llano Estacado, led by an Indian guide who intended to annihilate the expedition by getting it lost on the arid flatlands of West Texas. Although no one knows exactly where Coronado ventured, much evidence indicates that the southernmost point reached during the exploration was the North Concho River near present-day Sterling City, about forty miles from San Angelo.

The first non-native Americans who definitely came to the site of present-day San Angelo were Franciscan missionaries from New Mexico. They arrived in 1629 and 1632, at the same time English settlers were establishing the Massachusetts Bay Colony and the town of Boston. The missionaries came in response to Jumano Indians who claimed a mysterious "Lady in Blue" had told them to ask the priests for a Christian mission and protection from Apache enemies. The missionaries stayed with the Jumanos for at least six weeks, and perhaps several months, instructing the Jumanos and baptizing them in the Concho River.

Spaniards returned to the Concho confluence area in 1650 and 1654 to hunt bison, trade with Indians, and search for the distinctive Concho pearls produced by the freshwater mussels which gave the river its name (*concha* means shell in Spanish). In 1684 the Juan Domingo de Mendoza expedition camped at the Concho confluence for several days before moving east to establish Mission San Clemente in the San Sabá River country.

The Mendoza expedition was the last Spanish colonial effort along the Concho. During his exploration, Mendoza found evidence of French trade with the Indians, and a year later the remains of the La Salle expedition were found on the Gulf Coast, prompting Spain to focus its attention on East Texas and the San Antonio River. By the beginning of the eighteenth century, the Concho Country again belonged exclusively to Native Americans.[1]

Two hundred years later, people of Spanish-Mexican descent returned to the Concho Country as part of a pioneer wave penetrating West Texas after the Civil War. White men were already finding the Concho Country alluring by the time of the Battle of Gettysburg, and in 1864 a rancher named R. F. Tankersley established a spread at the head of the South Concho River.[2] Development of the region followed quickly thereafter. In 1865, George Washington DeLong started a ranch at Lipan Springs.[3] In December 1867, federal soldiers founded Fort Concho near the confluence of the North and South Concho Rivers. In 1868-1869, Jake Marshall began working the Bismarck Farm at the present site of Nasworthy Dam;[4] and at the same time, an ambitious entrepreneur named Ben Ficklin set up a stage line some three miles from Fort Concho.[5]

Most Mexican Americans came to the Concho

Country as day laborers in search of new opportunities. From 1868 to 1872, they comprised part of the crews of teamsters transporting supplies from San Antonio for use in constructing Fort Concho.[6] Mexican hay contractors cut prairie grass from the surrounding areas and furnished it to the garrison.[7] Mexicans also cultivated the fields at the Bismarck Farm, for Marshall had recruited them in his plan to feed the troops at Fort Concho.[8] Ficklin's stage line also relied on Mexican hands, and Mexicans worked on Ficklin's ranch land.[9]

Early Mexican Americans lived on ranches, but others made their residence in two fledgling towns: Ben Ficklin, located three miles south of Fort Concho, and Santa Angela, located on the North Concho, across the river from the fort.

A discernible rise in the number of Mexicans in the Concho Country occurred in the 1870s. Cattle drives that started around 1872, activity generated by Fort Concho's emergence as a central military base, the buffalo hide boom in 1874-1877, and the sheep industry established between 1877-1879 drew Mexican Americans to the area because each relied on their labor in some form or another.[10] By the first Tom Green County census in 1880, Hispanics made up twenty-four per cent of the county's 3,609 inhabitants. Some 268 lived in Santa Angela (designated as the "Town of Fort Concho"); 158 resided in a place called the "Town of Concho" by the census taker; another 200 lived in a village named Lone Wolf and in Ben Ficklin; the remainder lived on outlying ranches.[11]

Mexican activity in the Concho Country in the 1870s was not limited to low-skill work. Men who sought to acquire land, to make money, and to establish reputations had also immigrated alongside common men. Among these were families like the Alderettes, Camúñez, Flores, Subías, and others.

The Alderettes were the most prominent. Headed by Pablo Alderette, this family originated in New Mexico and arrived in the Concho Country from San Antonio about 1869 or 1870. They settled on land on the North

Concho and established a four hundred acre farm.

Don Pablo exerted considerable political influence in the affairs of the growing area. In 1872, for example, Alderette was sufficiently important in the affairs of Fort Concho that the military escorted his step-daughter, Catalina, and W. S. Veck to Fredericksburg, where the couple married.[12]

The Alderettes also were important in the area's social life. Don Pablo and Doña Ramona held dances which were attended by both Anglos and Mexicans.[13]

In addition to the Alderettes, the entire Mexican American community took an active role in the affairs of the Concho Country. In politics, it was their vote in 1875 that decided the location of the first county seat. As the story is told, Francis Corbett Taylor, the political leader in the town of Ben Ficklin, persuaded the Texas legislature in 1874 to create Tom Green County from Béxar County. Afraid that Santa Ángela might win in the showdown to determine where the county's administrative center would be situated, Taylor rounded up Mexicans from surrounding ranches and those employed by his stage line, then instructed them how to vote. A continued succession of Mexicans arriving in Taylor's stagecoaches on election day, January 5, 1875, gave Ben Ficklin the victory by sixty-five votes.[14]

Although this was an obvious case of "voting Mexicans," it was not exceptional to this period of American history when political corruption was common throughout the United States. In point of fact, those Mexican Americans with the ability and position to be assertive played a meaningful role in early county politics. Pablo Alderette made up part of the first County Commission in 1875 and was Justice of the Peace in his precinct.[15] His son, Guillermo Alderette, served on the first grand jury alongside three other Mexican Americans;[16] and, when the county was divided into justice and election precincts in late 1875, Guillermo's home was assigned as the polling place.[17] The first petit jury included four Mexican Americans, and Faustino Holguín was selected constable in Alderette's precinct.[18]

In the first years of the county's existence, Mexican Americans continued to make up parts of the grand and petit juries.[19] They also remained active at the ballot box. Thirty-five Mexican Americans voted in the first election, in February 1876, out of a total of 162 men who exercised the franchise. In one precinct, almost half of the forty voters were Mexican Americans.[20]

The early Hispanic presence in the Concho Country thus unfolded in two phases. The first included missionary activity and exploratory expeditions and covered a span of about 150 years. The second coincided with the American westward movement following the Civil War and this pattern of settlements proved to be a permanent one. Mexican Americans and Anglo Americans, therefore, arrived almost simultaneously along the Conchos and together brought the land under submission and built the city of San Angelo. Here, the Hispanic experience in the Concho Country was unlike that in San Antonio, where Anglos in the late 1830s penetrated an urban area already inhabited by Mexicans. It was also dissimilar in comparison to ranching areas of South Texas or the El Paso Valley, where Mexicans owned the land and had lived on it for generations before Anglos arrived in the 1850s and after.

CHAPTER TWO

The San Angeleños, 1870-1910

The town of San Angelo had its legal origin in 1870 when Bart DeWitt, a real estate promoter, arrived in the Concho Country to develop a town across the river from Fort Concho. Mexicans either already lived on DeWitt's land or moved on it immediately after his coming. They made their living by working around the fort, by tending cattle and doing similar chores on surrounding ranches or by servicing the soldiers with prostitution and drink.[1] During the 1870s, Mexican Americans made up the majority of inhabitants of the town.[2] It was they who called it "Santa Ángela," a name given to the settlement by DeWitt to honor his deceased wife, Carolina Ángela de la Garza.[3]

According to the descendants of early Mexican American families and students of early San Angelo history, Mexican Americans settled along the banks of the North Concho River and on Concho, Twohig, and Beauregard Avenues, on lots which DeWitt had marked off in 1871. Many probably were squatters, but few people really concerned themselves with the Mexicans' presence. Santa Ángela was a struggling town; there was plenty of space for arriving Anglos wishing to establish businesses and homes; and many land buyers owned properties *in absentia* and did not know who lived in town. Also, there were not enough inhabitants in the town to force Mexicans to live in any particular section. Furthermore, DeWitt probably did not object—he may have empathized with his departed wife's kinsmen. Several Mexican American families had bought land from DeWitt legitimately.[4]

Santa Ángela quickly became a base town for casual ranch hands commuting to outlying ranches. Seasonal workers like sheepshearers and cattle drivers also left their families in town for safekeeping during sheepshearing or roundup time.[5]

In 1877, Santa Ángela became the possession of Marcus Koenigheim, a San Antonio businessman, when DeWitt was unable to pay interest on loans he had obtained from the San Antonio entrepreneur. Koenigheim's arrival in Santa Ángela in 1877 to promote his new acquisition brought more Anglos into the town, but the real estate developer concentrated his efforts on property along Koenigheim, Abe, David, and Kenwood Streets, west of those parts of town where Mexican Americans were entrenched.[6] Furthermore, there was enough room in the town for recent Anglo immigrants to be selective in the places where they wished to establish their households and businesses; the town was still not thriving. Thus, racial friction producing the displacement of Mexicans from their old homes may have been minimal at this time.[7]

The year 1882 was a decisive turning point for Santa Ángela—or San Angela as the growing Anglo population now called it. In August, the competing and more prosperous town of Ben Ficklin was destroyed by a flood, sending more Anglo settlers—including merchants, bankers, land developers, and family-oriented citizens—to San Angela. Shortly thereafter San Angela became the county seat, and in 1883, symbolic of the Anglicizing of the town, the Post Office changed the name of the town to "San Angelo."[8]

By the mid-1880s, significant developments occurred along streets where Mexicans had once lived. Concho Avenue became the hub of activity, especially east of Chadbourne. Similar construction occurred on Twohig

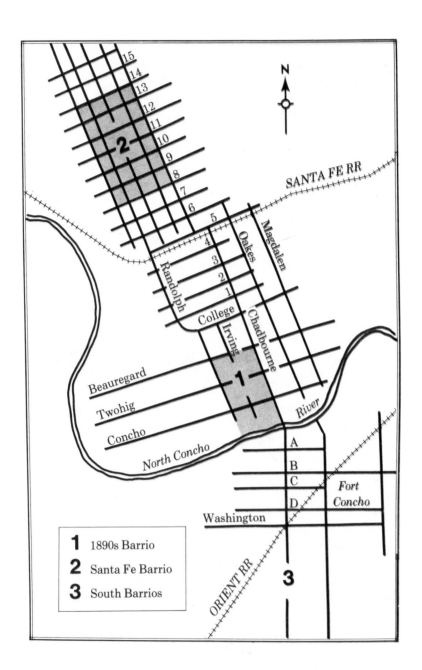

15
14
13
12
11
10
9
8
7
6
5
4
3
2
1

2

1

3

SANTA FE RR

N

Oakes
Magdalen
Randolph
College
Irving
Chadbourne

Beauregard
Twohig
Concho
River
North Concho

A
B
C
D
Fort Concho

Washington

ORIENT RR

1 1890s Barrio
2 Santa Fe Barrio
3 South Barrios

and Beauregard Avenues and on Chadbourne Street. In the process, the original Mexican claimants to these downtown lots were dispossessed—either bought out or forcefully evicted. Some Mexicans did cling to their lots in the area, however, and some may even have continued buying property.[9] Simultaneously, a pattern of ethnic separation emerged, and pernicious attitudes toward Mexicans were expressed openly. According to a Tennessee correspondent visiting the Concho Country in 1889, the Anglo Americans of San Angelo considered the Mexicans as "chiefly Aztec, with a sprinkling of Spanish and Negro," some of them "dark to the point of blackness."[10] Recent immigrants responding to calls for range hands in the late 1880s and 1890s[11] had to contend with these attitudes and their political implications.

The rapid growth of the town during this period escalated land values. Now real estate in the downtown areas, especially in the section north of Concho Avenue and east of Chadbourne, became coveted pieces of property. In the 1890s, Anglos began to displace Mexican Americans in this part of town, further restricting them to west Concho and Twohig Avenues and to the strip of land along the North Concho River. Some Mexican Americans profited from land sales, for they had acquired the lots at low prices. They valued cash more than real estate, failing to realize the inevitable appreciation of land values as the town grew.[12] Many Mexican Americans lost their holdings to prominent members of the Anglo establishment through fraudulent and unscrupulous means. Some of the lands in the downtown area where important buildings are situated today once belonged to Mexican Americans and passed to Anglo hands in questionable ways during the 1890s and the early twentieth century.[13]

By 1900, the Mexican American enclave in the downtown district was within a section bounded by Twohig on the north, Chadbourne on the east, the North Concho River on the south (though people lived along the river banks down to Oakes Street), and Randolph on the west.

At roughly the same time, the arrival of the Gulf, Colorado & Santa Fe Railroad spurred the beginnings of a second Mexican American settlement in San Angelo. The railroad reached San Angelo in 1888 (about the time that Mexicans were being removed from the downtown district) and passed through the northern perimeters of the city. Its depot was situated between East Fourth and Fifth Streets as they intersected with Chadbourne. The origins of this part of town went back to the aftermath of the Ben Ficklin flood six years earlier when various land speculators had come to San Angelo to begin anew. Among them had been Jonathan Miles, who sought the promotion of the northern part of San Angelo (from about today's College Avenue to 14th Street).[14] Experiencing difficulty developing the addition, Miles was compelled to sell lots at low prices. Mexican Americans working for the railroad, those working on nearby ranches and farms, and those being driven out of the downtown section found prices in the Miles Addition affordable. Anglos welcomed the migration across the railroad tracks.[15]

Mexican Americans initially bought property behind the courthouse, then purchased lots further north. The highest density of Mexican Americans homes was along Ninth through 14th streets on the west side of Chadbourne, an area Mexican Americans began calling *Santa Fe,* an obvious allusion to the nearby railroad.

Mexican Americans apparently concentrated in the Santa Fe barrio for several reasons. First, there was affordable real estate. Second, the area between 2nd and 8th streets, closer to downtown, developed as the black quarter, and there appears to have been an understanding that only blacks would live there—hence the distance of almost a mile from the downtown concentration of Mexican Americans and the Santa Fe barrio. Finally, other additions in San Angelo refused to admit Mexican Americans.[16]

By the early 1900s, there were two centers of Mexican

American activity in San Angelo—one declining in Mexican American population in the oldest part of town and another increasing in population in the northern part. In both places, the Mexican American culture bustled, endured, and evolved.

Hispanic San Angelo's First Families

Several Mexican American families were prominent in early San Angelo. Among them were the aforementioned Alderettes, who acquired lots in town from Bart DeWitt in the 1870s. It is uncertain exactly when the Alderettes moved to their new property; the 1880 census lists them as still living on Don Pablo's ranch. Mrs. Alderette and her children seem to have moved to their city property after Don Pablo's death in 1882. Mrs. Alderette soon became an integral part of San Angelo's Mexican affairs. So did Guillermo Alderette, Don Pablo's son by his first wife in New Mexico, and his family, who lived on West Twohig Avenue.[17]

The Wuertemburgs were another family important in early day San Angelo's Mexican American community. Catalina, Nestor, Charles, and Phillipi Wuertemburg were the offspring of Philip J. Wuertemburg, a German immigrant who died when the children were young, and Ramona Wuertemburg, his widow, who married Pablo Alderette during the Civil War.[18] The four children were carefully nurtured in Mexican American culture by their mother. All were bicultural, including Catalina or "Kate" (Doña Kattie in the Mexican American community),[19] who moved to San Angelo in 1872 when she married the town's leading businessman, W. S. Veck. According to the 1880 census, Charles and Phillipi also resided in town.

The Camúñez family followed the Alderettes and Wuertemburgs to San Angelo beginning in the late 1870s. Reynaldo Camúñez Sr. settled in the area after marrying Otilia Marquardt.

The Jesús Tafollas were another notable family.

Immigrants from Mexico, the Tafollas trekked their way to the Concho Country via San Antonio in the 1870s, and by 1880 lived in the city where Jesús Tafolla worked as a teamster.

The Félix Flores family came from San Antonio in quest of new beginnings in the Concho Country and settled in ranch areas west of San Angelo near Knickerbocker and Sherwood. By the mid-1880s, they had made their way to the city, settling to the south of the North Concho River.

A number of other families also were visible in the affairs of the Hispanic community of San Angelo before the turn of the twentieth century. Adolfo Varela was a man of some prominence beginning in the mid-1870s, judging from his regular inclusion in the original tax rolls. Félix Subía came to the Concho Country in time to serve on the first petit jury[20] and vote in the first county election of February 1876.[21] Antonio Flores, a painter who immigrated from Monclova, Mexico, in the late 1870s, was a close friend of Oscar Ruffini and painted many of the architect's West Texas buildings. While not joining the town's community until the 1890s, Florentino Muñoz contributed significantly to the welfare of Mexican American citizens.

Other families, about whom less is known, also made an impact on social life in young San Angelo. Among these were those of Fermín Corrales, Casimiro Girón, Fabián Navarette, Anastacio Marrujo, Gerónimo Sosa, Francisco Ronquillo, Inez Samarrón, Eufracio Estrada, Máximo Losoya, Andrés Jaramillo, Faustino Holguín, Isabel Cardiel, and Ygnacio, Florencio, and Clemente Morán.

Culture and Community

The social life of San Angelo's Mexican American community revolved around a variety of cultural affairs and entertainment forms. Some were traditions brought from Mexico. Other events came from the Mexican Americans' Catholic heritage.

Drawing Mexican Americans together in a common bond were *fiestas patrias* (national feast days). When exactly these dates came to be observed in the city is unknown; their earliest recordings are in 1885 when the Mexican population marked the *Cinco de Mayo* (Fifth of May)—the anniversary of the defeat of the French in 1862 by Mexican troops at Puebla, Mexico.[22] Two years later, another Mexican national holiday, the *Diez y Seis de Septiembre* (Sixteenth of September, which celebrates the cry Father Hidalgo issued for Mexican independence in 1810) was observed with a picnic and barbecue at Miles Grove on the North Concho[23]—a place that proved popular as a setting for fiestas patrias picnics thereafter.

In the 1890s, the formal aspects of the Diez y Seis commemorations were held at the hall of the Sociedad Fraternal Unión México Texana or at Pickwick Hall, a community building on Oakes Street, where dancing, orations, and patriotic displays showed the San Angeleños' link with their Mexican past. These occasions attracted diverse elements of the Mexican American community, among them invariably the members of the first families. Attending were the Corrales, Alderettes, Holguíns, Wuertemburgs, Muñoz, Varelas, Samarróns, Jaramillos, Tafollas, Camúñez, Flores, Subias, Estradas, and Ronquillos. Also present were Mexican Americans who had intermarried with Anglos—most prominently Mrs. W. S. Veck (Catalina Wuertemburg), Mrs. Walter Harris (Juanita Varela) and Mrs. James B. Keating (Jesusita Alderette), in addition to their children. Along with the rest of the Hispanic community, these people were instrumental in insuring the success of the fiestas patrias and carrying on Mexican American culture. Capping the celebration of 1894, for example, was a dance at the home of Mr. and Mrs. James B. Keating.[24] By 1910, the centennial of the declaration of independence from Spain, fiestas patrias commemorations were elaborate affairs in San Angelo, celebrated with much ado and fanfare.[25]

The social scene also embraced intellectual and

cultural presentations. In 1896, the Mexican Dramatic Company of the city performed in Spanish before a packed crowd at Pickwick Hall a laughable farce titled "In the Hilt of the Sword." Among the actors were members of the city's well known families, including the Tafollas, Flores, and Alderettes. The local paper praised Señor Pancho Holguín's direction of the play, lauded the acting, and commented positively on the beautiful and expensive costumes.[26]

In 1906, Mexicans of the city organized the Club Latino Americano. Its intent was to offer different sorts of social entertainment including the celebration of the fiestas patrias. The membership in this association also included prominent members of the Hispanic community like the Tafollas.[27]

Religious affairs occupied the serious side of life. Institutionalized Catholicism had arrived in San Angelo in 1880 when Father Mathurin Pairier built an adobe church on Beauregard between Chadbourne and Oakes Streets on property deeded to the Bishop in the mid-1870s.[28] In 1884 Father Pairier built Immaculate Conception Church at the corner of Chadbourne and Beauregard. There he ministered to Mexican Americans, who then represented the majority of Catholics in the growing town.[29] After 1906, Mexican Americans worshipped at the Church of the Sacred Heart, built at the southeast corner of the Catholic block at Beauregard and Oakes.[30] As more Anglo American Catholics established residence in the town, a policy of segregation developed in this church, and Mexicans were compelled to sit on one side of the building. Mexican American children attended Immaculate Conception Academy at the same place, but they also were segregated because of their national origin.[31]

Anglo observers in the 1870s and 1880s painted a disparaging picture of Mexican ways. Dr. William Notson, the post surgeon at Fort Concho remarked about the Bishop's visit to the city in 1871:

To complete the characteristics of wickedness and villainous traits with which the treacherous and dirty race [of Mexicans] abounds, where it is practicable to evade the fee and the Padre, even the simple ceremony of jumping a broomstick is evaded as a necessary preliminary to marital relationship. His Reverence put a stop to that, for the time at least, by marrying all or nearly all who had been living in such relations and very unwilling Benedicts most of them made.[32]

In 1889, Anglo citizens of the town told J. E. MacGowan, the Tennessee reporter quoted previously, that Mexicans had no particular morals concerning sexual relations, "except the mothers try hard to guard their daughters until marriage, or at least to the time of betrothal. Changing wives is not uncommon and neither partner has much regard for the proprieties when living together."[33]

Descendants of Mexican American "first families" and others who arrived in San Angelo in the first years of the twentieth century heard dramatically different accounts of norms governing morality during the initial decades of the city's growth. Marriage was a serious business, according to Mrs. Eva Camúñez de Tucker, a descendant of Reynaldo Camúñez, Sr. The task of asking for a bride's hand in marriage, for example, demanded a formal ritual and decorum. Eva Camúñez said of her parents' engagement in 1909:

Juan Flores vino a hacer las veces de padre cuando pidieron a mi madre [Josefa Lara]. En esos entonces traían una carta y se la daban, y le ponían plazo, se iban, y volvían.[34]

[Free translation] Juan Flores came to act on behalf of the [suitor's] father when they asked for my mother's hand in marriage. Back in those days they would bring a letter [to the bride's family]; a certain grace/decision period would be worked out; the groom's representatives would leave with an understanding to return at the end of the grace period.

Among prominent Mexican American families, thus, it seems there was much attention to morality and social form.[35] This atmosphere of esteem and cultural understanding resulted in several marriages between first generation children of the founding families. The Wuertemburgs married with the Camúñez, the Alderettes with the Tafollas, the Flores with the Marrujos, for example.[36] Additionally, several Anglo Americans married Mexican women in the 1880s and 1890s, and these included more than the well-known unions of Catalina Wuertemburg and W. S. Veck, Juanita Varela and Walter Harris, and Jesusita Alderette and James B. Keating.[37]

In the early years of the twentieth century, Turn Verein Hall, 132 East Concho Avenue, became the scene for social gatherings such as wedding receptions.[38] This hall seemingly was acquired through the good will and influence of Doña Kattie Veck. San Angeleños, thus, managed to secure a place on the east side of Chadbourne Street for cultural affairs, even though they were segregated to the west of it by that period.[39]

Tenacity

The political role played by San Angeleños and other Mexican Americans during Tom Green County's early years waned rapidly in the 1880s. Representation on juries ceased altogether, according to jury lists published regularly in the San Angelo *Standard* in the 1880s and 1890s. The loss of political presence may have been due to demographic factors—while Mexicanos were numerous enough to wield power in the political structure in 1875 and 1876, shortly thereafter Anglo newcomers who resented their participation swelled the city's white population. This placed San Angeleños in a difficult situation—their degree of involvement depended on the nature of their contribution to the local scene. Anglos permitted Mexican Americans to vote on certain terms; if, for example, political leaders stood to gain by using their vote.[40] Political independence or organized attempts to express conviction, on the other hand, met hostile reaction. This is what happened in July 1886 when the Tom Green County Democratic Party convention in San Angelo refused to recognize a large delegation of Mexicans. Delegates concurred with rancher J. R. Nasworthy, who presented a resolution that no one be allowed at the meeting who could not speak "the United States language." As the convention was cleared of Mexican Americans, the Anglo delegates applauded.[41] After the 1880s, disfranchisement became a general pattern for Mexicans.

Limitations notwithstanding, Mexican American political activity continued. For instance, thirteen Mexican Americans, including the familiar names of Alderette, Samarrón, Wuertemburg, and Casimiro Girón, Eufracio Estrada, and Fabián Navarette, were among 170 men petitioning to disincorporate San Angelo in 1904.[42] This effort to overturn the previous year's incorporation failed, however, and it is from 1903 that the city's legal existence dates.[43]

Segregation, discrimination, disfranchisement, and other practices that deprived Mexicans of a full measure of equality did not totally disrupt the orderly function of the community, for San Angeleños devised means of providing for themselves. Self-help societies, for instance, acted in lieu of mainstream institutions when the latter failed to serve Mexican Americans. With initiation fees and monthly membership dues, *mutualista* (mutual benefit) societies assisted their members in times of need, offered low-cost funeral privileges, and provided other financial succor. Among the first of the associations was the San Angelo Fraternal Union, founded in 1887 by Francisco Holguin, Eustacio Camúñez, Félix Flores, and others.[44] In 1899, there existed a Sociedad Fraternal Unión México-Texana which additionally sponsored or subsidized the celebrations of the fiestas patrias.[45] In 1909, the Obreros del Universo, a fraternal order similar to the Woodmen of the World, chartered a lodge in the city known as Taller No. 5. It had enrollment of twenty-six members.[46] A Masonic society also existed in 1910.[47]

Whether Spanish-language newspapers existed in San Angelo is unknown. In 1906, however, Señor Amado Gutiérrez of Del Rio arrived in San Angelo with plans to establish a weekly by the name of *El Liberal.* Copies of the paper do not exist, and the fate of the paper is undeterminable.[48]

As for the early educational facilities for San Angeleños, they seem to have reflected the general tone of attitudes toward Mexican Americans. From what can be gleaned from the 1880 census, education itself was not well advanced. The overwhelming majority of school-age children in 1880 did not attend school, and in the "Town of Fort Concho," of some ten children indicating that they attended school in the last six months, half were Mexican Americans. In the outlying areas of the city more Anglos than Mexican American children went to school. The children of Pablo Alderette, for instance, were among those attending classes in the country areas. Children of the first Mexican American families apparently also studied alongside Anglos in the subscription schools of the 1880s. A picture taken in 1884 shows a Mexican American student among the Anglos.[49]

These tolerant attitudes, however, yielded to a demand for segregation. According to one Anglo witness:

> For a time the Mexican had to attend the white school and such names as Jesús and Joe Tafoya, Hersails, Hernández and Minuel López; Billie, Relia, Albert, Ihas and Antonio Alderette; Juanita, Tomasita, Cecilia and Jose Coralis; Juan and Joe Flores, were very

familiar to the lower grade children. But they
only attended for a few years, for the citizens
early realized they should have a building of
their own. Mrs. Steffins did much for the
Mexicans and was a splendid teacher of theirs
for a number of years.[50]

By the 1890s, a "Mexican school" definitely existed
under the subscription system: in 1895, it was under the
tutelage of Kattie Veck, presumably a daughter of Kate
Veck, although her tenure as schoolteacher apparently
was short.[51] In 1896, the Mexican student population
was placed at sixty[52] and the number remained more or
less the same under Señora Ella Balencia (1902-1904)[53]
and Mary Veck (1904-1906), another daughter of Doña
Kattie.[54] The formation of the San Angelo Independent
School District in 1903 did little in the way of improving
conditions for Mexican American students, who
continued to be segregated.[55] The location of the
separate school was apparently moved around—some
sources put it behind the courthouse, others on Eighth
Street[56]—but it was normally situated where students
of the downtown district and those of Santa Fe had
convenient access to it. In 1910, the number of Mexican
American students eligible to attend the separate school
was approximately two hundred.[57]

It was the issue of education for Mexicans that
produced the first major confrontation between the
Anglo majority and the Hispanic minority in the city.
The problem arose out of the School Board decision in
early 1910 to provide Mexicans with an old frame
building abandoned by Anglo students transferring to a
recently finished schoolhouse. Led by Florentino
Muñoz, the Mexican community protested, and in June
a committee comprised of Muñoz and other Hispanic
leaders confronted the Board with demands for
admission of the Mexican American children to the
Anglo schools or the location of separate schools on the
same grounds. Conceding that the condition of the
Mexican school left much to be desired, the Board

Hispanic San Angelo—1910

• Indicates Hispanic household

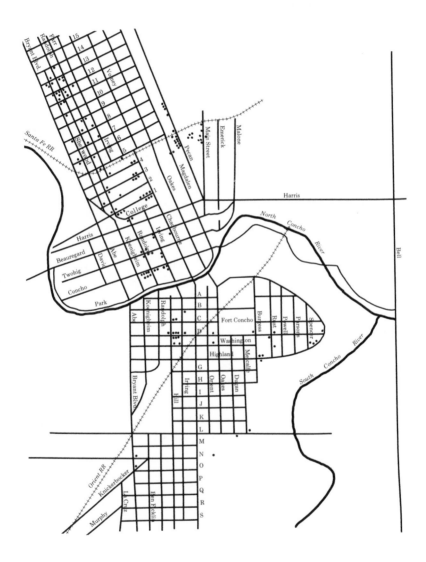

agreed to improve it to a level equal to the Anglo schools but absolutely refused to consider a policy of integration. Mexican Americans threatened legal action but the Board made no concessions.[58]

When the school doors opened on September 19, 1910, only two Mexican American pupils appeared at the two separate schools designated for their use. The boycott continued throughout 1910. Parents sent their children to Immaculate Conception Academy[59] and in subsequent years to the Mexican Presbyterian Mission school which opened in 1912. Things did not return to the pre-boycott days until 1915 when enrollment in the separate Mexican school matched the earlier figures.[60]

As of 1910, the Hispanic population of San Angelo was still small. The census takers of 1910 listed about 750 people of Spanish surname—about seven percent of the city's entire population of 10,321. Although the number of Mexican Americans had increased since the first census of 1880, the city's overall population had increased so much that the percentage of Mexican Americans in the city dwindled to a small minority.[61]

According to the 1910 census, forty-five percent of the 750 Mexican Americans lived in the Miles Addition, with the majority of these living between 6th and 14th Streets. Sixteen percent still lived in the downtown section and a small number lived in scattered parts of town. Now, however, one-third of San Angelo's Mexican Americans lived in the area south of the North Concho River. In succeeding years, this southernmost concentration would become the hub of Mexican American activity.[62]

CHAPTER THREE

A New Barrio Appears
1909-1929

By the early 1900s, a few Mexican American families already lived along Hill and Irving streets as they intersected with Avenue C, Avenue D, and Washington Drive (then called Avenue E). Among them were old-line families like that of the widow Justa Flores, her sons Juan and José, Casimiro Girón, Máximo Losoya, Antonio Flores, as well as descendants of other early settlers like the Navarrettes.[1] The forces that spurred the shaping of the southern barrio are difficult to discern. By the 1910s, however, the area rivaled the Santa Fe barrio in attracting new arrivals in San Angelo.

One factor was the coming of the Kansas City, Mexico & Orient Railroad in 1909—the railroad purchased land for its depot on Avenue D and Chadbourne from Juan Flores in 1910.[2] Second, and perhaps more significant, was the continued importance of the local sheep and cattle industries. The region's experimentation with cotton farming, furthermore, enticed Mexican Americans to the area, and a majority chose to live in south San Angelo.

Calls went out yearly from local ranchers for *tasinques* (shearers). The greatest demand occurred from March through May when goats were being sheared and the kidding season and the wool clipping were under way, while there was less urgent demand around September when some sheep were clipped a second time.[3] During World War I, the labor shortage became acute, and according to the United States Bureau of Immigration, shearers from Mexico were made available for West Texas ranchers.[4] Locally, men who supplied part of this labor were *enganchistas* (recruiters) like Juan Flores in the 1910s and his brother José Flores who ran the Flores Labor Agency on Concho Avenue in the 1920s.[5]

A similar demand for cotton pickers came from farmers each season. Though the Concho Country did not rely on cotton as a major staple, the crop was large enough that the local labor force was inadequate. "Cotton pickers are exceedingly scarce in the Concho area," reported the San Angelo *Standard* in October 1909, and "farmers in the Wall neighborhood need cotton pickers [in view of the fact] that there are few negroes [*sic*] in Tom Green County."[6] By the 1910s, area farmers were so desperate for cotton pickers that they sought workers on the streets of San Angelo.[7] Additionally, farmers urged chambers of commerce along the border to send surplus Mexican labor to the Concho Country.[8] Contractors throughout the state heard the petitions and promised to gather work crews.[9] Cotton pickers recruited from Mexico supplemented the local labor supply.[10]

Apparently, many of those who arrived in San Angelo as shearers and farm workers stayed in the town. But why did workers settle in the southern barrio during the 1910s and 1920s? Other than the railroad, no other major industry existed south of the North Concho River to draw Mexican Americans to this neighborhood. Discrimination apparently played an essential role in the formation of the southern enclave.

Early in San Angelo's development, real estate men had observed a policy of restricting Mexicans from certain parts of the city. Jonathan Miles had sold to Mexicans, but the Santa Fe barrio was situated "across the tracks," and housing patterns were confined. By the

Hispanic San Angelo—1920

• Indicates Hispanic household

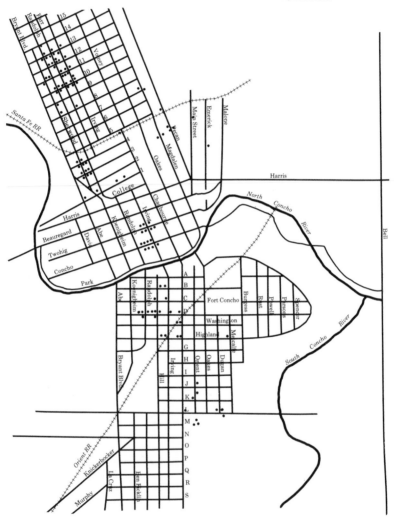

1910s, developers openly advertised the areas surrounding the Miles Addition as being for whites only.[11] As space grew scarce in the Santa Fe barrio, the Fort Concho Addition provided an alternative for settlements. White San Angelo during this period was in the throes of demographic expansion into all areas of the city save those "set aside" for Mexicans or blacks.

By 1920, the initial collection of homes around the Orient depot had grown into a neighborhood that encompassed homes in the area bounded by Avenue D, Randolph, Highland, and Chadbourne. By then it had taken on the name of *Oriente* among the Spanish-speaking residents—after the Orient railroad—to distinguish it from the Santa Fe barrio across town. In the years that followed, homes spread south, eventually reaching Avenue N. This appendage of the south barrio took on the tag of *Bulto Prieto* (Dark Figure).

Religion Comes to the Barrio

Throughout the 1910s, Mexican American Catholics of the city continued worshipping at Sacred Heart. By the next decade, however, the church was giving thought to establishing a second house of worship in the growing south barrio. The result was the founding of St. Mary's Church on Avenue N and Chadbourne in 1930.[12] Underlying these plans, Mexican American old-timers maintain, were attempts to rid Sacred Heart of its Mexican parishioners and segregate them permanently. In fact, St. Mary's was served by priests and nuns out of the downtown structure.

Protestant sects proselytized aggressively within the predominantly Catholic Hispanic population. Among these were the Presbyterians, who arrived in the city in 1912 and established a mission school with the goal of ministering to the students boycotting the segregated city school. The school was located in the 200 block of West Avenue E (Washington Drive) and administered by the Reverend Narciso Lafuerza, a Spaniard transferred from Havana, Cuba, and Mrs. Jennie Suter, remembered by the Mexican American population in the barrio as "Misure" (pronounced like "Missouri"). The efforts of Lafuerza and Suter produced the organization of the First Mexican Presbyterian Church in 1915.

The mission school itself, with some seventy youngsters by the mid-1910s, stressed the learning of the English language, held special programs at Christmas time and closing exercises in May, and, in time, expanded to offer free night classes for male students of any age. The school burned down in 1921, but efforts were quickly initiated to rebuild. For the rest of the decade, the Mexican Presbyterian Church and school remained visible fixtures in south Angelo.[13]

Mexican Baptists were equal to the Presbyterians in their ministerial zeal. They arrived in the mid-1920s and held summer camp meetings and Bible institutes on the outskirts of town. By 1928, the Baptists had moved into San Angelo proper, and were holding services and winning converts at their tabernacle on West Washington Drive. Behind the organizing skills of Donato Ruiz, Mexican Baptist missionary, the Mexican Baptist congregation grew to such a point by 1929 that a new church building was built at the corner of South Irving Street and Avenue L. In the 1930s, Ruiz turned to Radio Station KGKL to spread the word of the Baptists.[14]

Strides in Education

Historically, educators in San Angelo assumed that the schooling of Mexican Americans should be in segregated buildings and limited to the elementary level. Segregation had been the school board's objective in 1910 when it moved to provide two schools—one for children residing north of the Santa Fe railroad and the other for students located south of the river. This segregationist policy had been resoundingly rejected by the aforementioned boycotters.[15]

Despite their displeasure with the city's position,

Mexican Americans made their way back to the Mexican school by the middle of the 1910s. The Mexican school was now situated at 210 West Avenue A between Randolph and Hill streets—an apparent concession to the growth of the southern barrio because previous schools for Mexican Americans had been located in the northern part of the city. By May 1916, the Mexican school had an enrollment of about fifty students.[16]

The city Mexican school, however, was not the only outlet for students desiring an education. Indeed, this was the time when the Mexican Presbyterian Mission school was expanding—by May of 1915, it reported seventy-two students enrolled, though its average attendance was forty-five.[17] Simultaneously, the Catholics ran St. Joseph's school, and among those attending were children with names like Corrales, Holguín, Tafolla, and Wuertemburg.[18] As of 1918, St. Joseph's had a regular attendance of about fifty-two.[19] In the early 1920s, Mexican children also attended the Catholic Church's Immaculate Conception Academy, where they were taught in a two-room frame building behind the Academy. The school later was moved to 320 West Avenue D and called San Pedro.[20]

It was to the public schools, however, that Mexican Americans most often turned for their education, although they generally did not enroll in full force until December, after the cotton picking season ended. By 1922, educators were seriously considering expanding school facilities to accommodate the number of Mexican American children.[21]

The expansion did not materialize immediately. The inaction had little to do with lack of Mexican American enthusiasm, for the number of teachers assigned to the Mexican School—located at 1105 Farr Street in the mid-twenties—kept increasing. Among those who served during this time and who are remembered affectionately by Mexican Americans were Mrs. Roberta Parks, the principal, and Miss Ruth Rich, who continued her career in the Mexican school until her retirement in the 1970s.[22]

By the late 1920s, the school board could hardly fail to notice the steady rise of the Mexican student population. From ninety-five in January 1926, the number of students in the Mexican school had jumped to nearly two hundred by the spring of 1928.[23] The school board announced the opening of two new schools that fall. One was named the South Mexican School, situated at Avenue M and Ben Ficklin Road; the other was the North Mexican School, located at 11th and Randolph. In 1936, the names would be changed to Sam Houston Elementary and Guadalupe Elementary, respectively.[24]

After years of inconvenience, Mexican American students finally had the benefit of attending schools close to their homes. The location of the new schools testified to the demographic patterns of the city—the North Mexican School could be found in the middle of Santa Fe barrio, which had not grown much from its early boundaries, while the other school had been moved almost a mile farther south, indicating the rapid growth of the southern barrios. Attendance figures testified to sustained growth in the southern area. In February 1929, the total going to the South Mexican School was 205, and those enrolled in the North Mexican School amounted to 135.

Mexican Americans appeared to gain greater access to education with the opening of the schools— enrollment increased by about 120 between February 1928 and February 1929.[25] In truth, however, they faced the same obstacles as before. Children still tried to learn in a system that practiced a "separate but equal" policy and assumed Mexican American education should not go beyond the elementary levels.

Cultural Continuity

The grandest fiestas patrias heretofore held in San Angelo took place in 1910, the hundredth anniversary of the *"Grito de Dolores."* A parade of some 300 people on floats and buggies, including the San Angelo Military Band, initiated the two-day festival at Lake Concho Pavilion. Bunting, flowers, American and Mexican flags, evergreens, and paintings of Benito Juárez, Miguel Hidalgo, and Porfirio Díaz adorned the grounds. Patriotic songs, recitations, orations, and declamations filled the air. José Flores, a labor agent, and son of the old settler Félix Flores, was a prime mover in the celebration. Flores continued playing a leading role in the patriotic fetes until the 1930s.

With increased immigration, the fiestas patrias grew in size. By the mid-1920s, their organization followed a systematic pattern: each year the Mexican Government called upon a *Comisión Honorífica* (honorary commission) to convoke the Mexican American *colonia* (colony) which in turn appointed a *Comité Patriótico Mexicano* (Mexican Patriotic Committee) responsible for organizing the fiestas. The 1925 Cinco de Mayo celebration was one of the largest attended and most successful in San Angelo's history. It featured participation by second-generation San Angeleños like Eva Camúñez and Josefa Flores, the involvement of families who had arrived in the early years of the twentieth century like the Jaimes and Navarrettes, plus a new group of younger people. The same thing was manifest in the Diez y Seis commemoration that year, held on an open-air platform at 327 West Eighth Street and at Picnic Bend near the intersection of West 14th Street and the Concho River.

Towards the latter years of the 1920s, the enthusiasm of those settling in the southern barrios drew the festivities toward that part of town. Both the 1928 Diez y Seis and the 1929 Cinco de Mayo were staged at the end of South Chadbourne Street. Nearly 1,000 celebrants listened to José Flores and a new generation of fiesta promoters—among them Francisco V. Juárez, Máximo Guerrero, and Estanislado Sedeño—praise the glory of Mexico and pledge allegiance to the United States.[26]

The Barrios' "Other Face"

There was, also, a seamy side to San Angelo's Mexican American community in the 1910s and 1920s. This was not exceptional; evil has historically plagued civilized man, and Santa Ángela had been born amid a reputation of lawlessness and immorality.[27] Vice by no means decreased during the city's transition to the modern age. Although, banditry ceased to be a problem of the Concho Country frontier by the 1880s, a red-light district continued to thrive downtown until the 1920s.

Saloons, of course, have long been settings for vicious crimes, and indeed the bars along Concho and Twohig Avenues in the early days were scenes for notorious crimes. Guillermo Alderette was killed in an altercation with an Anglo watchman at the Corner Saloon in 1891.[28]

In the early years of the twentieth century, Mexican bars like the Corner Saloon, Coney Island, and the Grey Mule Saloon remained a stage for violent arguments, cutting affrays, and fist fights along West Concho and Twohig Avenues. In 1906, a barroom fight with an Anglo cost the life of Antonio Alderette, one of Guillermo Alderette's boys. This was the first murder in San Angelo since 1902, reported the *Standard*.[29]

In the period between 1910 and 1925, crime increased in the Mexican American section. The scenes were primarily the center of town—in the old barrio where Mexican American saloons, restaurants, barbershops, labor agencies, and the like were located. The area apparently was not well policed,[30] a reflection of the city's traditional relations to ethnic enclaves.

The central barrio and its surrounding blocks were the settings for more than a dozen murders, countless stabbings, and lesser crimes during this period. These were not limited to bars, though saloons were among those places where men with grudges and other evil motives squared off with malicious intent.[31] Eating establishments had their share of episodes involving knives and firearms, and two deaths were recorded in 1922 involving arguments between customers and the proprietors. In both cases, the victims were shot several times by the restaurant owners they were assaulting.[32]

The primary settings for bloody encounters, however, were the streets. Murders involving Hispanics took place on West Concho Avenue in 1911, 1916, 1919, and 1921, with only the latter case involving the killing of an Anglo.[33] Streets on both banks of the North Concho River drew others to their death. A long-standing family feud brought about the demise of the last of the Alderette boys when Pablo was killed at the corner of Avenue A and Hill Street in December 1912, and Ajeo was gunned down as he stood in front of a saloon at 227 South Irving in November 1913.[34] That block was also the setting of the era's bloodiest episode—the killing of José Tafolla, a successful businessman and scion of one of the early families. Police shot him repeatedly at 2:00 a.m., on September 6, 1925, as he took refuge in a small home on Concho and South Irving following a street altercation.[35]

Bawdy houses in the downtown barrio reflected another side of Mexican American life. The houses traced their origins to Fort Concho days; they had persisted in the latter years of the nineteenth century as female "boarding houses" and thrived in the 1910s on West Concho Avenue alongside the saloons. In the 1910s, reformers sought to clean up the city and the entire tri-ethnic red-light district came under attack. The social welfare commission investigating the situation in 1914 reported to the city council:

> There are six or seven bawdy houses located on West Concho Avenue, all of which are conducted in open defiance of our laws. The inmates of these houses are white girls numbering from twenty to forty, ranging from sixteen to twenty-five years of age. There are also several Mexican and negro [sic] houses of ill-fame, located on West Concho Avenue, and in close proximity to the white houses.[36]

The reforms seem to have been only partially successful, for Mexican American old-timers remember the homes existing years after the reform attempts.

Death of a Barrio

The vestiges of frontier days in downtown Mexican San Angelo faded in the second half of the 1920s. This was due in large part to the "modernization" of the city. In the previous decade San Angelo experienced a population decrease from 10,321 in 1910 to 10,050 in 1920.[37] More specifically, the change was due to the transformation of the downtown business district.

As late as the first years of the 1920s, the downtown barrio bustled to the extent that Anglos thought of it as a village within a city—unique in its culture, customs, language, and code of morals. A reporter from the *Standard* wrote in 1920:

> San Angelo has its "village" and well might it be termed "Little Mexico." West Concho Avenue at the intersection of South Irving Street is the center of the village. For a block's distance on all four sides the village extends and in these blocks there are several alleys cutting the regulation city blocks up into smaller sections. These alleys form the streets and every available space practically is covered by a frame house or shanty.
>
> There are small stores and restaurants. These form the downtown section of "Little Mexico" while on each side not more than a block away in each direction lies the residence district. Business is conducted just as is true in any village and to all intents and purposes it is separate and distinct from the city of San Angelo.[38]

But starting in 1925, this part of the city underwent a restructuring due to the West Texas oil boom. Many of today's buildings went up at this time, including the courthouse, the City Hall, the downtown churches, and the Cactus Hotel. The San Angelo National Bank, the Texas Theatre, and the Roberts Hotel were built closest to the old barrio.[39] The Sante Fe Park also was created, infringing on the southern edges of the enclave.[40] Families who had resided in the old barrio since the early days were bought out—among them Ricarda Alderette, who in 1927 sold the property her husband Guillermo had bought on Twohig Avenue. She moved to the Santa Fe barrio where she died a few years later. By the 1930s, only a few elderly families retained their earlier property, and a few Mexican American business places lingered along West Concho.[41]

CHAPTER FOUR

Depression and War, 1930-1945

The prosperity that transformed downtown San Angelo gradually dissipated during the early 1930s. By 1933, oil was overabundant and cheap, while farmers and ranchers suffered through a devasting drought. San Angelo's remaking came to a sudden stop[1] and with it a diminishing of jobs available to San Angeleños. By then, the city also felt the effects of the national depression.

Maintaining a reasonable standard of living was more difficult for Mexican Americans because Anglos saw them as competitors for precious opportunities. Xenophobia flared up when some suggested the country should reserve its limited fruits for native whites. Locally, this attitude surfaced in March 1930 when the Central Labor Union (CLU) of San Angelo publicly supported the restriction of Mexican immigration; it seemed to members that Mexican laborers found better opportunities for employment than "Americans." According to speakers at one of the CLU meetings, seventy-five percent of the men employed by two local paving contractors were Mexicans, and the same were doing a great deal of the city work.[2]

Strict enforcement measures adopted by federal relief agencies worsened things for Mexican Americans. In December 1933, relief officials announced that Mexican Americans would be eligible for Civil Works

Administration (CWA) projects only if they had been in the United States or had taken out naturalization papers before November 16, 1933. Such guidelines were particulary discriminatory for those who had never proclaimed their citizenship—many Mexicans had been brought across the Rio Grande as infants and had seen no reason to become naturalized—or for those who had been in the country only a short time.[3]

Open threats against Mexican American laborers further weakened an already frail material condition. In June 1931, for example, anonymous groups threatened Mexicans through letters to the chief of police and the San Angelo *Standard*. One letter to the head law officer promised raids on Mexicans in and around the city and was signed "The Unemployed—South with Mexicans." The letter to the *Standard* read:

> We are forming a club known as the Darts. Our aim is to clean up our city and make working conditions better for Americans. You will hear from us from time to time as our good work progresses. Each member will work separate not knowing any other member. All Mexicans must leave.
>
> Dart[4]

Reflecting a disturbingly casual attitude, the police treated the letters as pranks or crude jokes.

Mexicans also faced uncertainties that accompanied repatriation efforts across the country. In Texas, deportation of Mexicans was carried out with persistence, but there were no major drives in the sparsely populated areas of West Texas. In September 1931, however, some twenty Mexicans in San Angelo petitioned the Mexican government for assistance, pleading lack of finances for a return to the motherland.[5] Whether said persons were seeking relocation because of the above related threats or for other reasons is unknown.

Repatriation efforts emanated also from well-

Hispanic San Angelo—1930

• Indicates Hispanic household

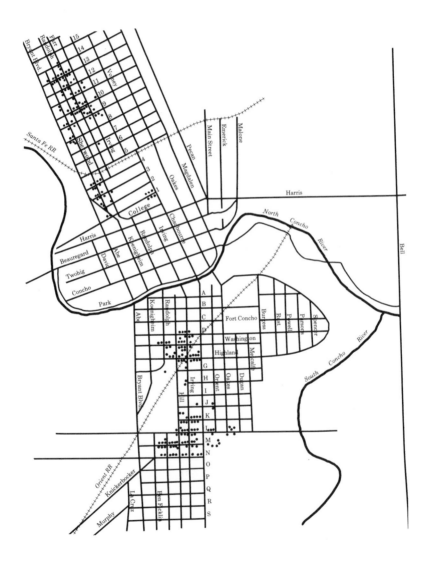

meaning Mexican American groups. In April 1939, for example, a San Angelo Committee for Repatriation of Mexicans sought to help Mexican nationals return to the homeland. Such committees were common in other Mexican American communities in Texas, existing under the guise of Comisiones Honoríficas, mutual-help societies, and Comités Pro-Repatriados. Such groups were designed to assist the Mexican government in helping economically distressed Mexican nationals return to Mexico.[6] Many of those considered for repatriation in San Angelo, however, owned residential property and other holdings and had children born in the United States.[7]

Mexicans were not completely barred from relief programs. A number of young men participated in the Civilian Conservation Corps (CCC),[8] and the Works Progress Administration (WPA) offered various types of assistance.[9] On some of these projects, however, Mexicans performed the more grueling tasks, while white laborers did the less taxing ones. Segregation in the ranks of public works relief was common.[10]

As if the Depression were not enough, there was also natural disaster that inflicted a toll on San Angelo's Hispanic community. For days in mid-September 1936, rains poured throughout the city, causing the Concho Rivers to overflow. The North Concho swept through the Santa Fe section, picked up houses and carried them onto other people's property or threw them against the Sixth Street bridge then under construction. In all, approximately forty families lost their houses at the intersections of Sherwood and Sixth, Seventh, and Eighth Streets.[11] In the southern barrios, residents experienced similar devastation. Many of the distressed families found shelter at St. Mary's Church, Sam Houston School, the Mexican Presbyterian Church on Washington Drive, and at an old Piggly Wiggly food store at Avenue K. Flood victims received food, clothing, and blankets courtesy of the Red Cross, the Salvation Army, and Anglo churches. Others found themselves isolated by the waters and compelled to sleep in their cars. Although the flood did $20 million in damage, no lives were lost.[12]

Resilience

It is difficult to determine the impact the above forces had on the size of the Hispanic population—about 2,500 in 1930.[13] Demographic growth in San Angelo was meager; the town increased by only 500 inhabitants between 1930 and 1940.[14] At first sight, it appears the Depression years either reduced the size of the Hispanic community or, at least, stifled expansion.

Neither may have been the case, however, for numerous factors indicate the census of 1940 does not provide an accurate count of the Mexican American population of the city. The cotton harvest, for example, regularly brought people to San Angelo on the "Big Swing" which carried farm workers from South Texas fields all the way to the Midwest. Each year, some of those workers were attracted to San Angelo and added to the local population.[15] Many of these people apparently settled south of Avenue N. This area, called *La Loma* (The Low Hill), extended to Avenue S in 1940 and consisted of about nineteen blocks, 125 to 130 houses and 625 to 650 inhabitants. Because this area was outside the city limits,[16] its population was included in the county census figures instead of the city's. Within La Loma there was a red light district immune from city patrolling; it was confined to a few blocks behind St. Mary's Church to about Avenue Q. It went by the sobriquet of *El Pozo* (The Pit).

The employment of Mexican American policemen to patrol the southern barrios further indicates the growth of the Hispanic population. By the early 1930s Hispanic law enforcement officers no longer were rare: Nick Peña, Mauricio Valadez, Joe Wuertemburg, and Frank Camúñez were among the new recruits.[17] Although residents were now protected by men who identified with Mexican ways, at the same time the employment of Hispanic lawmen helped institutionalized segregation. Mexican American policemen understood that they were to leave the white sections of town alone. Indeed, a major controversy would arise over precisely this restriction in the post-World War II years.

Self-Amelioration

Other activities in the community corroborate a mood of dynamism, assertiveness, and flux in the 1930s. The time was one of intensified efforts at self-amelioration, starting with the founding of a local lodge of the Alianza Hispano Americana (Hispanic-American Alliance) in the late 1920s. Brought to San Angelo through the efforts of the Tafolla family and other concerned people, the society sought to extend insurance provisions and other privileges to the city's Hispanic population. In September 1928, it held its formal installation at a hall on 13th Street and Farr. A traveling Alianza representative initiated some sixty members, including Inez Tafolla as president, José Martinez, vice president, Noé Fierros, secretary, and Dora Tafolla (sister of Inez) as treasurer.[18] The order took the name "Emilio Carranza Lodge" in honor of the Mexican aviator who died in a plane crash earlier that year. Dora Tafolla was crowned queen of the organization in May 1929.[19]

While the fraternal Alianza group avoided civic activities in the 1930s, such was not the case with the League of United Latin American Citizens (LULAC). Founded in February 1929 in Corpus Christi, Texas, LULAC aimed to arouse the political ambitions of Hispanics, to develop ideal Mexican American citizens, and to improve relations between "Latin Americans" and Anglos. In June 1930, it established a branch in San Angelo, though the local chapter—Council 27—apparently was not formally installed until the next year, when M. C. Gonzales of San Antonio arrived for the official ceremonies.[20] The Council's initial officers descended from the founding families—among them José Flores, president, and Inez Tafolla, vice president. The LULAC met at El Salón de la Prevención, 304 West Washington Drive.[21]

Council 27 took an activist role. One of its early cases involved the Social Security program created in 1935. According to instructions issued by the Social Security Board in 1936, Mexican Americans who applied for social security were to designate themselves as "Mexicans" instead of "whites." The San Angelo council, led by its vice president, José M. Rodríguez, took exception to the ruling and, along with numerous other LULAC councils throughout Texas, filed written protests with officials in Washington, D.C. According to the statement released by Rodríguez and Council 27:

> We are engaged in educational work designed to make our people conscious of their citizenship rights and obligations and duties. We are not ashamed of our blood heritage; in fact we are justly proud of the blood that courses through our veins. But we want to feel that we are not just a group of "Mexicans" but a vital part of the American people that make up this great nation in which we live.
>
> We cannot do this work effectively if an agency of our government is going to discriminate against us as to a separate class or group. We therefore, urge you revise your form and permit our people to be classified as 'WHITE.'

Politicians reacted quickly to Hispanic concerns, and the Social Security Board directed officials to disregard the designation on the printed form and to accept the application of Mexican Americans as "whites."[22]

The Supreme Court eventually dealt with the issue when it ruled that Mexican Americans were a special class of Caucasian race in *Hernández* v *The State of Texas*, 1954. The case arose when Pete Hernández was tried before an Anglo jury in Jackson County. G.I.

Forum attorneys argued that there was discrimination because Mexican Americans had not been part of the jury. The Texas Court of Criminal Appeals held that Mexican Americans were Caucasians, that the jury had been Causcasian, and Hernández was, therefore, tried by his peers. In overturning the decision, the Supreme Court ruled Mexican Americans were a separate class among Caucasians and that Hernández was a victim of discrimination.[23]

The San Angelo LULAC continued to fight discrimination in subsequent years. In November 1940, joined by the Ladies Council of LULAC, PTA's from Mexican American schools, the Mexican American Workers of the World, the Masonic lodges, and the Comisión Honorífica Mexicana of the city, Council 27 opposed the segregation of Mexican Americans reportedly planned for the Plaza Theatre. A resolution swiftly went to Latin American embassies in Washington, Texas Senator Penrose B. Metcalfe, and national LULAC officials. The management of Concho Theatres, Inc., which owned the Plaza, issued a statement arguing that in twenty-three years of service to the San Angelo community they had maintained a tradition of contributing to the well-being of Mexican Americans. Concho Theatres, the owners declared, had provided a movie house especially for showing Spanish-language films and had donated to Mexican American churches, celebrations, and organizations. Accommodation, not segregation, was the policy in all their theaters.[24] This statement was false, for Mexican Americans who lived through that era remember segregation existing in San Angelo theaters until well into the 1950s.

The LULAC protests of the 1930s and the war years were carried out while Council 27 carefully cultivated a reputation for Americanism. One of the League's aims, said E. D. Salinas, President General of LULAC, during a stop in the city in September 1938, was to "bring about an education of Americans of Latin extraction to such an extent that they will not be prey for the workings of Communism, Socialism, or other anti-American groups."[25] Hence, Council 27's many endeavors had a public-spirited ardor. The council sponsored fund drives for the Red Cross, backed the draft in August 1940, held patriotic dances, and participated in citizenship programs.[26] These projects were guided by descendants of the old families like the Cardiels, Tafollas, Jaramillos, and Losoyas, plus a new generation of activist leaders like Joe and Noah Valadez, Esequiel Duarte, George Jaimes, Albert Cano, and Henry V. Vélez.

Ad hoc groups, formed to protest specific incidents of prejudice, also contributed to the thrust towards social betterment. One such committee—made up of José Rodríguez, Pete Cardiel, Máximo Guerrero, and young Henry V. Vélez—in December 1936 and January 1937 inveighed against the proposed segregation of Mexican Americans at a public performance at the municipal auditorium by the Orquesta Típica from Mexico. On the logic that "Latin Americans" would enjoy sitting together, the San Angelo *Standard,* the show's sponsor, designated the auditorium's balcony for Mexicanos. Community leaders, however, saw the reservation of the upper level as a pretext for segregation. They contacted several of the Mexican consuls in the state as well as Mr. Ángel J. Mercado, the director of the orchestra. Mercado then threated to cancel the concert if the event was not integrated. The result was a public apology by the *Standard* and integration of the audience.[27]

Education

The 1930s witnessed further steps in the education of Mexican Americans. The two segregated schools continued their pattern of growth. By February 1932, the South Mexican School had increased by more than 100 since the late 1920s. The rise persisted throughout the 1930s. Each May—the month when the most Mexican Americans were enrolled—from 1935 through 1939 the enrollments were more than 550. This testified to Mexican American interest in education, but it also indicated the continued population growth in the southern barrios. Comparatively, the North Mexican School grew only by little more than 100 between 1929 and 1939.[28]

Enlightened, dedicated Anglos also participated in the educational advances in the barrios. Among these were Mrs. W. W. Carson, who led the fight for better facilities for Mexicans (and also founded the Fort Concho Museum);[29] Miss Ruth Rich, head of the South Mexican School; Roberta Parks, principal of the North Mexican School,[30] and teachers like Ruth Hillyer.

Hispanic advances became evident also in the post-elementary grades. Periodically, the local paper printed the honor roll for the junior high schools, and Mexican Americans appeared on the list occasionally, among them Luz López and Antonio Menchaca. By the late 1930s, more Mexicans were finishing junior high and going on to high school.[31]

It was also in the 1930s that the Hispanic community produced its first Mexican American high school graduate: Eva Camúñez, daughter of Mr. and Mrs. Reynaldo Camúñez, descendants of early city families. Undaunted by the implied rule that Mexicans should not attend the higher grades, Eva committed herself in the late 1920s to breaking the ethnic barrier. With the perceptive assistance of her parents, who had sent her to a San Antonio school, Eva presented herself at San Angelo High School with certificates showing her eligibility to continue further. In high school, she participated in several activities, including organizing the Spanish Club. In 1930, she became the first Mexican American native of San Angelo to graduate from the city high school.[32]

Others followed Miss Camúñez during the Depression years, though they comprised only a handful and often graduated alone. This was the case with Noé Camúñez (1934), brother of Eva, and Helen Robles (1935).[33] By World War II, however, the number of graduates increased. In 1940, Hiran Raúl (Roy) Enríquez,

Salvador Guerrero, and A. G. Menchaca graduated.[34] Others who succeeded were Ruth Ruiz in 1941, and Luciano Cano, Arthur Flores, Alexander Jaramillo, and Víctor Cardiel in 1942.[35] Rául Losoya completed his high school education at mid-term, 1942-1943.[36]

Religion

The Catholic Church maintained its growth through the 1930s. St. Mary's was the center for both religious and social life for the south barrios. The church grounds were the site for some fiestas patrias celebrations. After the 1936 flood, relief efforts were organized at the church.

The lack of a chapel in the Santa Fe barrio was rectified in 1936 with the building of a church structure at 1201 North Randolph. In the beginning, Mission San José, as it was called, was staffed by priests from Sacred Heart. This status changed in 1961 when St. Joseph became a parish.[37] The Catholic Church served most Mexican Catholics, but it also fostered a pattern of racial separation. Membership in Sacred Heart Church, for example, was limited to Anglos.[38]

The Mexican Baptists also continued their activities. Much of the Baptists' success was due to the efforts of the Reverend Donato Ruiz, who built up membership from practically nothing in the mid-1920s to respectable numbers in the 1930s. From his base in San Angelo, he traveled to surrounding counties and organized twenty churches with about 3,500 members and sixty missions by the early 1940s.[39] The local Baptist group periodically hosted district meetings, and received people from Kerrville, Brownwood, San Antonio, and other towns in West Texas.[40] When Ruiz left for El Paso in 1944, he was succeeded by the Reverend G. C. Rodríguez.[41]

The Mexican Presbyterians also served Mexican American religious needs. After years at 215 West Washington Drive, they purchased property on Avenue N, where a new sanctuary was dedicated in 1941.[42]

Other Protestant churches made their appearance in the city in the 1930s. A Mexican Methodist church was established in April 1938 and met at the home of Ismael O. Rodríguez on South Irving.[43] By the war years, the church had its own pastor.[44] Also originating in the early 1940s was La Iglesia Apostólica en la Fe de Cristo Jesús, Inc. (Apostolic Church in the Faith of Christ Jesus), which held its first services in its tabernacle on South Chadbourne and Avenue K in May 1944. Its pastor was Fabián Pacheco.[45]

Fun and Games

The Club Recreativo Cuauhtemóc, designed to organize outings, picnics, and other social activities for young men and women, and La Unión del Pueblo Latino Americano, a civic organization, observed the fiestas patrias celebrations at El Salón de la Prevención, 304 West Washington Drive, in the early Depression years. After this, the fetes were led by a new generation of men like Francisco V. Juárez, Máximo Guerrero, and Estanislado Sedeño, members of the Comisión Hohorífica during the decade. Under their guidance, several elements characterized the fiestas: these included coronations, national costumes, parades to City Hall to invite city officials to the grounds at St. Mary's Church, visits of consuls from other Texas cities, baseball games, sack races, similar activities. Crowds ranged from 2,000 to 4,000 people. During World War II, the organizers used the occasion to contribute to the war effort, and celebrants in 1943 bought some $1,000 worth of bonds and stamps at the festival site at the Community Gym, 203 W. Concho.[46]

Mexican American athletes emerged during the 1930s. The Black Tigers[47] were among several popular baseball teams. Distinguished amateur boxing careers were fashioned by Joe Flores Jr., descendant of Félix and Justa Flores and son of José Flores, the labor agent,[48] and Noah Valadez, whose best years were in the late thirties and early forties.[49] Hiran Raúl (Roy)

Enríquez was among the first Mexican Americans to gain attention for his feats as a high school track star.[50]

G.I.'s

Like most Mexican Americans throughout the United States, San Angeleños took a keen interest in World War II and gave resounding support to the war's objectives. One of the first expressions of these sentiments came in August 1940 when LULAC Council 27 joined other district chapters in supporting the Burke-Wadsworth Bill, which intended to implement a military draft.[51] Once the United States entered the war in December 1941, numerous local youths saw combat—including Alexander Jaramillo, Moses Moya, Noah, Jimmy, and Joe Valadez, Paul, Luis, and Eliseo Zúñiga, Fidel García, Gilberto Vélez, and Nestor Wuertenburg III.[52] Pedro Morán and Pedro Rivera were killed in action.[53] Pedro and Domingo Zúñiga, Joe Náñez, and Pedro García were killed in France in 1944,[54] and their bodies were not returned to San Angelo until several years later.[55] Others like Rito Renovato spent years in prison camps.[56] Willie Garza was captured at Corregidor or Bataan in the Philippines in May 1942 and spent the next three years as a prisoner of war. Garza was released in September 1945, but he spent another year in Burns General Hospital in Santa Fe, New Mexico, before being furloughed in November 1946.[57]

Ajeo Alderette

Antonio Alderette

Guillermo Alderette

Angela de la Garza

Mexican Americans picking cotton in the Concho Country about 1910.

The Morales family in front of their San Angelo home about 1910.

The Bastardo family in front of their San Angelo home about 1900.

Otilia Marquart Camúñez, flanked by her sons, Reynaldo (left) and Frank. Her daughters (in front, from left) included Emilia, Katy, Lola, Angelita, and Maria; about 1915.

Students and teachers at the San Pedro School.

St. Mary's School in 1950s.

Immaculate Conception Church about 1900.

Sgt. Joe Tafolla Jr.   Sgt. Hiran Roy Enriquez

Fiestas Patrias pageant and celebration at Fort Concho, 1984

Mexican American students, 1950s

Mexican American protest rally at Tom Green County Courthouse, 1978

Members of the Junior G.I. Forum in the 1950s

Ed Idar, attorney

*Armando Figueroa,
city councilman*

Wilma Figueroa,
homecoming queen

Eva Camúñez-Tucker,
first graduate

Maria Cardenas, city councilwoman

Tenna Arteaga,
1984 Miss San Angelo

CHAPTER FIVE

The G.I. Generation in Years of Flux, 1945-1959

Determining the number of Mexican Americans in San Angelo at the end of the war is difficult. One barrio resident quoted in the *Standard-Times* estimated that the Hispanic population had risen from 6,000 in 1941 to 9,500 in 1945. Of these, 3,500 resided within the city limits, he believed, the rest lived in the peripheral areas south of the town.[1]

Such estimates were high, but there had been substantial growth. Many of San Angelo's Mexican Americans lived in the county areas beyond Avenue N. For community leaders, the problems of the unincorporated areas were a major concern because of the lack of police protection, sanitary facilities, lighting, streets, education, and the like. Attempts to improve conditions was their primary goal during the post-war years.

Annexing "La Loma"

At the end of World War II, San Angeleños who wanted to improve living standards achieved a long-dreamed goal—the hiring of Mexican American peace officers to patrol in south San Angelo. The change began in August 1945 when a delegation of Hispanics presented their desire to the Tom Green County

Hispanic San Angelo—1940

• Indicates Hispanic household

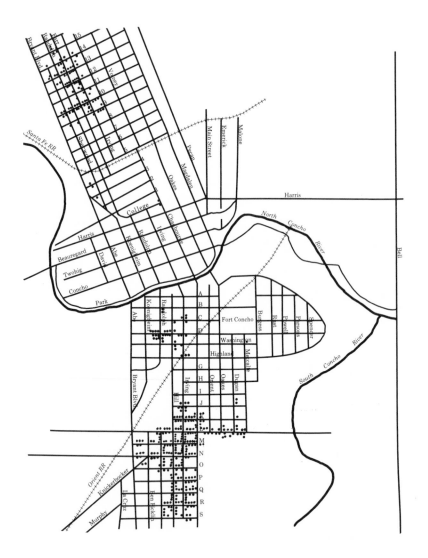

Commissioners' Court. The delegation included Albert Cano, owner of Little Mexico Restaurant; Mrs. Aurora García, wife of a soldier; Ezequiel Duarte, a radio mechanic; and several other barrio residents, including priests and ministers.[2]

Although the commissioners agreed to hire a Mexican American officer, they initially proposed to limit his duties to the barrios and to allow him to arrest only Mexican Americans. San Angeleños reacted strongly against the discriminatory limitations, and after several meetings the problems were solved. Cleto Ponce was then named deputy sheriff with the same rights and obligations as his Anglo counterparts.[3]

Three months after the County Commission episode, the delegation of Mexican Americans visited the City Commission and asked that a policeman be hired to work in the southern barrios alongside Ponce. At the same meeting, Mr. Cano, Mrs. García, and others asked about procedures for extending the city limits from Avenue N to Avenue S.[4]

Annexation of the southern barrio was the second major objective for Mexican Americans seeking better living standards in the latter 1940s. In January of 1946, proponents of annexation circulated a Spanish-language leaflet publicizing the benefits of extending the city limits to Avenue V. The leaflet argued that annexation would bring city police patrol, a larger public school, bus service, improved sanitary conditions, a sewer system, gas, and street lights.[5] Within days, the number of signatures required to petition the City Council for annexation had been recorded.[6] In spite of the enthusiasm, various problems delayed annexation until September 1949.[7]

The issue of annexation confirmed south San Angelo's standing as the center of Mexican American life. Increasingly, the important community leaders came from the southern neighborhood. The fiestas patrias celebrations were held along Avenue N. In 1950, a new school, Río Vista, was built at 2800 Ben Ficklin Road. It was from the south side also that drives to end segregation and discrimination were launched.

Discrimination and Protest

Editor of *Standard-Times:*

After reading in the San Angelo *Standard-Times* on July 24, [1945] the list of five West Texas towns where discrimination for Latin-Americans exists, as reported by the Mexican Committee at Austin, the Latin-American citizens of San Angelo wonder why San Angelo is not included in that list.

The fact that discrimination exists in San Angelo for the Latin-American citizens cannot be denied. Too numerous to mention are the cases where Latin-American citizens have been refused service in cafes, drugstores, etc.

In spite of the fact that Latin-American citizens pay taxes, they are not allowed to use the municipal swimming pool or the gymnasium.

Our Latin-American born are found in every theatre of war. Our Latin-American boys are not segregated at the front line. They are fighting right beside the Anglo American boys. They are dying beside the Anglo boys for a most worthy cause—that democracy may live and so that people may have all the privileges of a democracy.

After the Latin-American boys return to their loved home and they find that they are not considered good enough to go into a cafe because they happen to be of Mexican origin, how will they react? How will they feel to know that they have not the same rights as their Anglo American buddies?

The mothers and wives who have sacrificed the lives of their loved ones to win the war—how do they feel when they are refused a glass of water in a cafe? Their children are not good enough to enjoy the rights of American citizens, but they are good enough to die defending their country. The Latins will feel just like the Jews in Germany.

If Latin-Americans in Texas are not to be "The Jews of Germany" then discrimination should be completely abolished and Latin-American citizens should be allowed to exercise all their privileges as given to all citizens by the Constitution of America.

My brother and my brother-in-law are in Okinawa. My own husband, Fidel Garcia is now in the Medical Corps in India, where he has been serving for more than two years, and I feel very keenly about what I have said and I feel that I have a right to say it.

Respectfully,
Mrs. Aurora Garcia,[8]
205 Avenue S,
San Angelo, Texas

Mrs. Garcia, age 23 when she wrote the letter, was a leader among Mexican American activist women. She had supported annexation of the southern barrio; she had lived in the city much of her life; and she had experienced discrimination in the city firsthand. Her poignant letter spotlighted a problem of constant concern to Mexican Americans.

Up until the 1960s, when the monumental case of *Brown v. Board of Education* (1954) began having effect, Anglo society in San Angelo found it hard to totally separate from old attitudes toward Mexicans. Segregation remained a rule of race relations and Mexican Americans were perceived as second class citizens, much as they had been since the town's founding. In the downtown area of San Angelo, for example, Mexicans were denied service in most of the eating establishments during the war years, even when some wore their military uniforms.[9]

The personal harassment of Mexican Americans also

continued. Hazing and other forms of provocation were as evident against Mexican Americans in the summer and fall of 1945 as before. Boys and girls were cursed by Anglo teenagers or were harassed as they walked the downtown streets.[10]

The most infamous case of victimization involved the beating of a young war veteran by eleven Anglo teenagers on September 1, 1945. The causes for the assault are unclear. The Anglo boys (ages 16-17) claimed the twenty-year-old ex-soldier and two companions had cursed at them as the Anglos drove by in a pickup on South Chadbourne. The Mexican Americans then allegedly threw something at the pickup, whereupon the Anglos dismounted from the vehicle and beat the ex-serviceman.[11] Residents of the barrio believed the Anglo boys were out "hunting greasers" just for fun and that the violence was unprovoked.[12]

The serviceman required brain surgery as a result of the beating, and the Mexican American community was outraged. The San Angelo Ministerial Association passed a resolution deploring "this un-American and despicable act by a gang of Anglo American youths." Three barrio church leaders, and Albert Cano, J. M. Jácquez of the Mexican Grill, and José Figueroa of Figueroa's Grocery, telegraphed the governor of Texas, the Mexican consul in Austin, and Mexico's Secretary of Foreign Affairs, stating:

> We ask for your sincere cooperation. For some months past, there has been an organized gang operating in San Angelo, Texas, composed of Anglo Americans who have been and continue to threaten, abuse, beat, maltreat, and waylay Latin Americans. One example being that of [a young military man] who was beaten into unconsciousness and has been in such a condition in the local hospital for the past week. We respectfully request that you forthwith dispatch as many Texas Rangers as

possible to put a stop to this practice. Delay in bringing this condition under control will undoubtedly be fatally serious. This condition has been known to local authorities for some time. Your prompt action in this matter is urgently requested.[13]

Reflecting the newspaper's lack of news sources in the San Angeleño community, the *Standard-Times* did not report on the controversy until a week later, when Mrs. Aurora García informed the editors personally. Laudably, the newspaper immediately published stories about the incident and was so revolted by the episode that it editorialized: "This incident is a blot on the escutcheon of the city of San Angelo, and on the respect that some non-fighting elements of our citizenry owe to some other who, to some degree, at least, donned the uniform of the United States soldier."[14] The veteran ultimately recovered. The Anglo youths were arraigned in juvenile court.[15]

The G.I. Generation

For Mexican Americans who had earnestly devoted their war energies to eliminating oppression, the beating case was a painful reminder of the way some parts of Anglo society perceived them in San Angelo. Speaking out against racism was not new for San Angeleños. After World War II the voices were those of the new generation which had been touched by the principles of the war; many were veterans of the fight against totalitarianism.

Among those in leadership roles were men like Henry V. Vélez, Frank A. Martínez, Máximo Guerrero, Joe Valadez, and José Figueroa. For these men, discrimination and inequality lingered as a blot to be erased from the San Angelo environment. To this end, they organized a new LULAC chapter—No. 152—in 1948 to provide the unity needed for the social betterment of Mexican Americans.

Segregation especially raised their ire, since so many of the veterans had been exposed to tolerant conditions overseas. Eating places remained notorious for excluding Mexican Americans. In April 1948, for instance, members of two San Angeleño families were refused service at an ice cream parlor on North Chadbourne with the terse statement that "We don't serve Mexicans here." A policy of prohibiting Mexican Americans existed at the municipal swimming pool.

LULAC leaders brought these conditions to the attention of city officials and also appealed to the Good Neighbor Commission in Austin and to officials in Mexico. On other fronts, LULACers sought to encourage people to pay their poll tax, get the city to erect traffic signals, and light up heavily traveled streets such as Avenue N. They also took a special interest in education. LULAC Council 152 investigated stories of discrimination in the public schools. Sam Houston students were not allowed to participate in the Little Olympics, for instance. They protested sanitary facilities at Sam Houston, where outside toilets were in appalling shape, and they pursued the idea of having the school district sponsor evening classes to teach citizenship and English.[16]

In spite of these important LULAC activities, it was the American G.I. Forum that emerged as the organization for the times following the war. The Forum was founded in 1948 in Corpus Christi by Dr. Hector P. García to protest poor medical care received by veterans, the lack of proper financial benefits for Mexican American servicemen, and discriminatory treatment Hispanic veterans received from Anglo veteran groups. The Forum also reflected patriotism instilled by the war. Forum members recited the pledge of allegiance at meetings, proudly wore caps fashioned after those worn during the war, and reiterated their commitment to making the United States a better place for Mexican Americans.[17]

In San Angelo, mistreatment of war heroes—veterans found credit hard to acquire, counseling services were unresponsive, the employment office expressed disinterest, and job training was not forthcoming[18]—became an impetus for founding a chapter of the G.I. Forum in September 1948. The formational meeting was held at the Acapulco Club on South Chadbourne; Dr. García was the main speaker. As veterans, García asserted, Mexican Americans had won their rights and now intended to have them. "We must have the rights now for which our Latin American soldiers were drafted and killed in a fight to preserve them," he said. The G.I. Forum was committed to seeing that Mexican Americans voted, he added, and drives would be made to see that people used the ballot box. The first officers of the San Angelo G.I. Forum included Oscar Caballero, president, and Joe Valadez, vice-president.[19]

The Forum was the leading force in the betterment of living standards in the Mexican community during the 1950s. Forum leaders included many who had membership in LULAC Council 152, which faded during the early fifties. Leaders included Henry V. Vélez, Máximo Guerrero, and veterans like B. C. Domínguez. Their efforts were directed toward getting paved roads, lighting, sewers, and running water in the barrios. The men also led back-to-school programs and poll tax drives. To get local officials to respond to barrio needs, they took their grievances to the city council, dispatched delegations to visit groups discriminating against Mexican Americans, pressed for the end of police brutality, and sought outside assistance from G.I. Forum officials to handle legal issues.

The leaders were supported by an active Junior G.I. Forum comprised of Edison Junior High and high school students. Teenagers like Cato Cedillo, Pete Chapa, Ed Bernáldez, Delia Guerrero, Pilina Guajardo, and others raised money by sponsoring dances, raffles, and golf tournaments to assist needy residents of the barrio who had suffered eviction, needed emergency hospital care, or were unable to pay utility bills. By the late 1950s, this cadre of junior forumeers had become members of the Senior G.I. Forum and continued with the goals of improving conditions in the barrios.[20]

Years of Flux

Few Mexican Americans were immune from prejudices lurking in San Angelo in the post-war era. It touched Dr. José Benutto of Monterrey, Mexico, when he stopped at a San Angelo cafe in 1950 on his way to Littlefield, Texas, where he worked. The waitress refused him service on the grounds of his nationality. Anglo San Angeloans later tried to make amends for the embarrassing incident by holding a large banquet in honor of the Mexican physician. City business and professional leaders apologized publicly and explained that the refusal had been made by a newly hired curb-service girl on the job for the first night. They assured the doctor that this was not typical of the way San Angelo treated Latin Americans.[21]

The fact that the city went out of its way to apologize to Benutto reflected a changing climate for race relations in San Angelo. By this time, the city—like much of the country—already felt awkward about its treatment of minorities. In 1943, for example, the governor of Texas established the Good Neighbor Commission in order to improve relations with Mexican Americans. Claude Meadows of San Angelo, a member of the commission, stated at the Benutto banquet:

> I believe our national and state governments are now making the most determined efforts they have ever made to improve relations with Latin America, and I believe the current relations between the United States and the Latin American countries are the best in history.[22]

The persistent demands of LULACers and Forumeers also weighed on Anglo minds, so that in the 1950s, San Angelo found itself having to juggle a position somewhere between extremism and the movement toward reforming racist ways. The city's response was thus understandable, when in early 1951 the national magazine *Look* published an article titled "Texas' Forgotten People"—an exposé on the treatment of Mexicans in the state. Focusing on San Antonio, the article accented the tuberculosis problem among Mexican Americans, unsanitary living conditions, neglected schools, discrimination in restaurants, and the "wetback" problem throughout Texas. "Nowhere else in America is a group of people so downtrodden and defenseless, and nowhere are human dignity and life held in such low regard [as in Texas]," the *Look* article maintained.

The magazine story was denounced by San Angelo's Human Relations Council as being composed of half-truths and rebutted with the assertion that the conditions described did not apply to San Angelo. If the tuberculosis rate in the city was high, the infirm contributed to it, since many came to the Concho Country for the climate and living conditions, one member argued. The wetback question was a state and federal problem, not a local one, noted another.[23] The *Standard-Times* wrote that education was being given increased attention in the barrios, as witnessed by the recent construction of Rio Vista Elementary School. Moreover, students were being encouraged to continue their education in college.[24]

The city newspaper's offensive went further. It offered ten dollars for the best letter expressing appreciation for the United States and gratitude for opportunities offered in Texas. Another ten dollars would go for the best criticism of Texas and the plight of Mexicanos, with suggested remedies.[25]

The responses were numerous. Sergeant Noah Leyva of Goodfellow Field asserted that he had known discrimination firsthand, but that it was on the decline.[26] The prizes, however, were won by sixth-grader Evelyn Guevara, who voiced her appreciation for America, and by high school senior, Frances Ponce, who commented on the problems of Mexican Americans. Others writing included Preciliano Gallegos, Mike Terrazas, Jesse Leija, Juanita Samarrón, and Inez O. Hernández. The essays, though candid in their criticism of prejudice, expressed the theme that things were heading for the better, not for the worse.[27]

School Days

These writers were aware of problems besetting the areas in which they lived, so their comments testified to a fresh optimism emanating from the sense that things were in flux. In schools, for instance, conditions and attitudes were no longer what they had been during the time when education was for Anglos only. By the late 1940s, Sam Houston was overcrowded and Mexican Americans were bused across town to Guadalupe Elementary school in the Santa Fe barrio. The school board opted for busing instead of sending Mexican Americans to Santa Rita and Fort Concho schools which were closer but had a "whites only" policy.[28] The founding of Rio Vista Elementary School permitted the school officials to end busing and continue segregation, but it also afforded Mexican Americans greater access to educational opportunities. As a result, the number of Mexican Americans enrolled in the city's public schools increased.[29]

Also during this time the school system hired its first Mexican American administrators and teachers. The principal at Sam Houston between 1950-1953 was Noé Camúñez, a descendant of one of the first families.[30] Antonio G. Álvarez taught at the same school about the same time.[31] Jesús Barrera, a music instructor in the public schools from 1957-1962, was a University of Texas graduate who took an active role in city cultural affairs, including playing with the San Angelo Philharmonic Society.[32]

At Edison Junior High, 112 North Magdalen, Johnny Chapa was elected as vice-president of the student council in 1956. His election was somewhat of a coup since Mexican Americans in that period comprised less than fifty percent of the student body. Victory was achieved through the concerted effort of Chapa's Mexican American peers who campaigned tirelessly on his behalf. Chapa's brothers, George and Lorenzo, also served as student council officers in subsequent years.[33]

Mexican Americans also pursued higher education. Raymond M. Holguín graduated from San Angelo College in 1951,[34] and Juanita Samarrón did likewise in 1956.[35]

But it was at San Angelo High School where education was most gratifying. The number of graduating Mexican Americans had been increasing since the war's end,[36] and in the fifties the high school on Oakes Street became a common learning ground for many with roots in the barrios. The class of 1958, for example, included 23 San Angeleños in a class of 301 graduates.[37]

The 1950s also saw the first generation of Mexican American high school sport standouts. The spotlight beamed brightly on three basketball players—Elias Menchaca, Frank Treviño, and Albert Miranda. In the mid-fifties, their names seemed to be in every sports section of the *Standard-Times* as they led their team to victory in several important games. Treviño and Miranda continued their careers at San Angelo College, where they led the junior college to a national championship. Both finished their college and basketball careers at Sul Ross State College.[38]

The most symbolic achievement of Mexican Americans in high school was the election of Wilma Figueroa as queen of the 1958 Homecoming football game.[39] What might have been unthinkable in San Angelo just a few years earlier now materialized. It seemed a fortuitous way for Mexican Americans to start off things at the newly built Central High School.

Religion and Community

Religious denominations concentrated their work in

the southern areas of the city during the post-war years. The Assembly of God Church was located at 2400 Hill Street[40] and the Church of Christ, which began its work among Mexican San Angeleños in 1946, built a church at 2510 Ben Ficklin Road.[41] The Mexican Presbyterian Church, which for decades had been situated on Washington Drive, moved to 313 West Avenue N.[42] The Latin American Methodist Church was at 1900 S. Hill Street.[43] St. Mary's Catholic Church remained at Avenue N.

Several churches took active parts in civic affairs. Antonio Guillén, pastor of the Methodist Church until 1947, and Father Raymond Soper of St. Mary's were among the leaders in the annexation movement.[44] Along with G. C. Rodríguez, pastor of the First Mexican Baptist Church, they endorsed the telegram sent by the Mexican American community to the governor after the beating of the Mexican American serviceman in September 1945.[45]

Although most churches centered their efforts in the southern barrios, the Catholic Church did not forsake its faithful in Santa Fe. Mission San José, the little church established on North Randolph, was in the throes of expansion by the early 1950s. In 1953, Fray Fidelis Albrecht initiated efforts to build a new church structure on 17th Street and North Randolph. Through the efforts of parishioners who donated their time and energies by soliciting donations to purchase materials, holding fundraisers, and working on the church building themselves, the new church was finished and dedicated in November 1957. Mission San José's architectural design was that of the early day missions of the west. It had a church on the north side, living quarters across the back, and a hall on the south. It was surrounded by a high stucco fence with a courtyard in the middle.[46]

Las Fiestas Patrias

From 1945 to some thirty years thereafter, one man

came to symbolize the patriotic link San Angeleños had with Mexico. His name was Estanislado Sedeño, a native of Mexico who became a part of the city and the celebration of the fiestas patrias in the 1920s. Sometime in the mid-forties, he became president of the Comisión Honorífica, and from 1950 until his death in 1974 the fiestas patrias were celebrated in front of his home at 113 West Avenue N.

In the 1950s Sedeño and members of the Comité Patriótico Mexicano shaped the fiestas into an event that rivaled other gala affairs held in the city. Members of the Comité solicited contributions and donations from business firms and supporters of the Mexican American community in order to finance the fiestas patrias. They set up food booths, prepared the public announcement system, extended invitations to dignitaries, organized the parades, and established the program. Each year, San Angelo was treated to the two-day Cinco de Mayo and the three-day Diez y Seis celebrations. Great pomp and circumstance inaugurated the festivities each May and September. The crowning of the queen—a ritual generally performed by the mayor of the city—culminated each celebration.

On September 16 of each year, a huge parade of floats, convertibles carrying the queen and her entourage of duchesses, flag carriers, girls dressed in various Mexican costumes, troupes of performers from México, the Comité Patriótico Mexicano, the Lake View High School majorettes and band, and the Goodfellow Air Force Base drill team and band made their way from Sedeño Plaza down Abe Street toward City Hall, where civic clubs, city officials, and North Angelo Mexican Americans were invited to join the procession. Then the caravan turned south on Chadbourne Street where eager supporters usually awaited.

The fiestas patrias attracted such large crowds that police blocked off the street in front of Sedeño Plaza. Eventually, the space in front of Sedeño's house could not accommodate the throngs at the celebrations. In

1956 the local paper observed that "Saturday night, the 100 block of Avenue N looked like a segment of a plaza in Mexico, as the Latin Americans here started the Diez y Seis de Septiembre." The fiestas patrias became significant enough that invitations to participate in the ceremonies were accepted by San Angelo College president Dr. Raymond Cavness, State Senator Dorsey Hardeman, Representative O. C. Fisher, and the Goodfellow Air Force Base commanders. Visitors from Mexico, including congressional representatives from the state of Coahuila, mariachi bands from Ciudad Acuña, and consuls from other parts of Texas accepted invitations from the Comité Patriótico. Programs featuring recitations, patriotic speeches, folk dances, confectionary and food stands around the plaza and along the street, pageantry, and nightly dances blaring music for several blocks around the plaza colored the festivities of the 1950s.

In an era when the country was caught up in McCarthyism, when Operation Wetback made house-to-house raids for illegal aliens, when reactionary forces repressed civil rights movements almost with impunity, when Jim Crowism continued to segregate Mexicanos from Anglos, Don Estanislado and the Comité Patriótico raised the fiestas patrias celebrations to pinnacles of success in San Angelo. Due to the ability of the Mexican American community to extract concessions from Anglo society, to leaders committed to retaining their Mexican heritage, and to the dominant society's willingness to use the fiestas patrias as a "safety valve" for the diffusion of potential trouble from the Mexican American community, Sedeño Plaza became a focal point for the socio-cultural gatherings of a community rallying behind a common heritage.[47]

Korea

Less than a year after the body of Pfc. Pedro García, killed in the Normandy invasion, was returned to San Angelo for reburial, Rubén G. Bara, of 218 West Avenue

D, met death in Korea.[48] Several other San Angeleños responded dutifully to yet another call to arms. Some returned as decorated veterans, others did not come back. Among those who met the same fate as Bara were Tranquilino Pérez[49] and twenty-one-year-old Alberto Hernández.[50]

CHAPTER SIX

New Horizons, 1960-1968

In 1960, San Angelo had a population of 58,815.[1] It was a city in pursuit of progress. People were experimenting with one-way streets in the downtown district, pressing for a four-year college, expanding to the southwest part of town, and conceding to a changing age of race relations by finishing the integration of its public facilities and schools. As the city pushed toward new horizons, so did its 8,000 citizens of Mexican descent.[2]

The City Commission Races

In 1958, Henry B. González visited San Angelo during his campaign for governor. Then a Democratic state senator from San Antonio, González drove into the city in a low-priced station wagon to establish a campaign staff locally. At the old Mexican Grill, 1623 South Chadbourne, he breakfasted with leading Hispanic San Angeloans, including Armando Figueroa, Henry V. Vélez, and Máximo Guerrero. His goals as governor, he told a reporter, would be to revise the tax fund allocation system, enact youth conservation projects, find solutions to urban problems, inaugurate state programs to cut unemployment, control narcotics addiction, and deter brucellosis in Texas cattle. At noon that day, González went before a Rotary Club luncheon to push his campaign objectives.[3] He returned in later weeks to campaign, but his efforts eventually failed and Price Daniel was reelected.

The González campaign, however, increased the visibility of Mexican Americans who would grasp political openings in the 1960s through the early 1970s. Henry V. Vélez was a long time activist, had belonged to LULAC since the late 1930s, and had joined the G.I. Forum in the 1950s. Máximo Guerrero, who arrived in San Angelo in 1926, had long assumed a civic role, and was known about the community as a dance promoter and radio personality on station KTXL. Armando Figueroa ran a grocery store at 226 West Avenue N, sold real estate, was a member of LULAC Council 152, donated money and merchandise to barrio projects, integrated the Santa Rita Housing addition by purchasing a house on Jackson Street, and won respect for his polished manner of politicking in both languages. Others who took a noticeable role in Hispanic politics of the era included B. C. Domínguez (a World War II veteran and city police officer), Evelio Villarreal, Pete Chapa, Ed Bernáldez, and Cato Cedillo. All five were G.I. Forum members.

Aristeo Canales Jr. was the first Mexican American to run for a city office in the 1960s. A native of El Paso, the twenty-six-year-old Canales was a San Angelo College graduate who married a local girl while stationed at Goodfellow Air Force Base; he sold insurance for a living. In May of 1960, Canales filed for a vacant spot on the City Commission contested by seven other candidates. Canales, however, was handicapped by his status as a newcomer to the city, and he gained only 122 votes out of 2864 cast—but two others received even fewer votes.[4]

San Angelo's Mexican Americans were politically disadvantaged in 1960. Without substantial Anglo support, a Mexican American candidate could not win, even if every Mexican in the city paid a poll tax, registered to vote, and turned out on election day.[5]

Futhermore, San Angelo's political structure worked against Canales. Traditionally, the San Angelo political establishment has been more loosely organized than the political machines and organizations elsewhere. Anglo business and professional leaders wielded the most power, in contrast to settings where politicians exerted authority commensurate with their posts.[6] Lacking approval of Anglo power brokers, Canales had no chance of victory.

Armando Figueroa—City Commissioner

Armando Figueroa, who was known and respected by the Anglo power structure, was in a better position to win election when he cast his name for Place 4 of the city commission race in 1962. Campaigning on a moderate platform calling for industrial expansion, downtown parking, street lighting, closer cooperation between city agencies, and a full-time city planner, he forced a runoff election in April by coming in second in a three-way, at-large race. When he defeated the opposition a month later, he became the first Mexican American to be elected to the city body.[7]

Born in Cuatro Ciénegas, Mexico, Figueroa moved to Del Rio, Texas, as a child, and was naturalized at the age of twenty-one. He moved to San Angelo after World War II. In 1962, he was president of the Southside Lions Club, a member of the Tom Green County Welfare Board and the Tom Green County Tuberculosis Association, and a director of the Board of City Development. Previously, he held positions on the San Angelo School District Advisory Committee and on the Executive Board of the Citizens Progress Committee.[8]

Figueroa had extensive connections with Anglo businessmen and professional leaders through his civic work and his real estate business. In the barrios, Figueroa's efforts in behalf of Mexican Americans also won him solid support.

Philosophically, Figueroa walked a middle course during his tenure in office. He recognized that his association with Anglos was an important part of his victory, and that militancy and over-aggressiveness spelled failure. Since Hispanics were numerically weak, they did not have a chance of making the kind of impact that would change the status quo. Thus, the pragmatic Figueroa was not overly vocal or aggressive in his advocacy of Mexican American rights.[9]

Figueroa stood for reelection in 1964 on a platform which noted his experience of the last two years, the need to have a Mexican American on the commission (although he carefully explained: "I represent all the people, not any special ethnic group"), the desire to complete unfinished tasks, and the urgency of having paved streets in the barrios.[10] Figueroa again took his candidacy to civic groups, service organizations, and businessmen, as well as to Mexican American neighborhoods. This time he was elected without a runoff.[11]

In 1966, when Figueroa decided not to run for reelection, Ed Idar Jr., a local attorney, sought Figueroa's old spot, Place 4 in the at-large race. Son of an activist family from Laredo,[12] Idar had been in town since 1962 and pointed to his numerous contributions. He had been on the board of the Family Counseling Service, promoted Adult Basic Education classes held in the San Angelo public schools, lobbied for the conversion of San Angelo College to a four-year institution in 1963, and supported the Boys Club, YMCA, United Fund, and Heart Association.[13] Though acquitting himself well among the voters, Idar lost,[14] partly because of a whispering campaign which stressed his membership in the Political Association of Spanish-Speaking Organizations (PASSO) before coming to San Angelo.[15] Some considered PASSO a radical group.

New Professionals

The figures of Canales, Figueroa, and Idar were reflective of the growing number of civic-minded businessmen and professionals assuming a more strident role in San Angelo politics. Idar had received his law degree at the University of Texas Law School and had practiced his profession in Laredo and McAllen before opening up his office at the old Central National Bank building at 30 South Chadbourne Street. During World War II, Idar served in England as a civilian at an Eighth Air Force support facility. He returned to the United States and joined the army in 1944; he served in India and China and was decorated with the Bronze Star. A typical member of the "G.I. Generation," Idar joined the G.I. Forum in 1949 and was its second state chairman.[16]

Evelio F. Villarreal came to San Angelo in 1959 and three years later opened up the first complete drug store to serve the barrio south of Avenue N. Villarreal served in a medical corps unit in the African and Sicilian campaigns during World War II and had been a German prisoner of war. After the war he received his degree from the University of Texas School of Pharmacy, and worked for a San Angelo pharmacy, then moved to San Angelo and established his own pharmacy on Ben Ficklin Road. Villarreal's interests extended toward civic matters. He was a director of the Southside Lions Club, a member of the Knights of Columbus, and belonged to the G.I. Forum.[17]

Dr. Robert Martínez arrived in San Angelo in 1963 to become one of the few Mexican American physicians in San Angelo's history. A native of Rotan, Texas, Martínez took his medical studies at the University of Texas Medical School in Galveston; he began his first practice at 201 East Beauregard in San Angelo.[18]

The leadership of San Angelo's Mexican American community in the 1960s consisted of a coterie of small bussinessmen, war veterans, participants in the González gubernatorial run of 1958, supporters of Armando Figueroa, and professionals recently arrived in the city. Many of them belonged to the American G.I. Forum, the most activist Hispanic organization of the era.

Taking Umbrage

In January 1962, a letter to the *Standard-Times* warned:

> Wake up, you white Anglo people, and pay your poll tax. The Mexican population is getting more numerous and could take over. Someone said in your paper not long ago that it was a shame to have a man named Gonzales representing the San Antonio district when an Anglo candidate could have been elected.[19]

Pilina Cedillo, a member of the Ladies Auxiliary of the G.I. Forum, responded by noting in a letter to the editor that Mexican Americans fought for the United States just like Anglos did. She continued "we do not want special rights in this country, all we want are the privileges we are entitled to and have fought for, like equal representation in government."[20]

The tone of Mrs. Cedillo's letter to the editor reflected the vigor of the G.I. Forum, then enjoying its heyday in San Angelo. Besides conducting poll tax drives, the local chapter initiated new programs such as sponsoring a yearly tiny tots dance, holding Christmas parties for disadvantaged children, and granting sports awards for Hispanic Central High School athletes. The Ladies Auxiliary and the Junior G.I. Forum assisted with the programs.[21]

The San Angelo chapter's success in getting the state organization to hold its convention in San Angelo in 1963 further testified to the strength of the G.I. Forum in San Angelo. At the same time, Ed Idar Jr. was the State Executive Secretary of the Forum and, in that capacity, used his influence to bring the convention to his home city. In keeping with the group's patriotic image, the Fourth of July was chosen as the beginning date for the three-day meeting. Organizers included such well known civic activists as Cato Cedillo, Pete Chapa, and Ed Bernáldez, plus younger men like Richard V. García, Mario J. Cruz, Johnny Chapa, and

Ray Moya, and teenage women like Adelita Gonzales, Yolanda Moya, Christine Tafolla, Corina Enriquez, and Elva Escoto.[22]

The state convention proved a coup for the local organizers when it was attended by several people who hold a significant place in Mexican American history. The dignitaries included Raymond Telles, former mayor of El Paso and then ambassador to Costa Rica; Raul Morín, author of *Among the Valiant,* an important book on Mexican American participation in World War II and Korea; and Dr. Garcia, founder of the G.I. Forum and a tireless crusader for Mexican American rights. Other eminent personalities included Chris Aldrette and James DeAnda, recognized as central figures in the shaping of the early Forum.

The Most Reverend Thomas J. Drury, bishop of the San Angelo diocese and chaplain for the Forum, held mass for the delegates at Sacred Heart Cathedral early on July 5, and city councilman Armando Figueroa welcomed the Forumeers in behalf of the city. Keynote speeches during the course of the convention were delivered by Dr. Garcia, who praised President John F. Kennedy for his appointment of Hispanics to federal, ambassadorial, and commission posts; Morín, who expressed optimism for an improved future for Mexican Americans; and Telles, who discussed the boundary dispute over the Chamizal area of El Paso—officially settled during the Lyndon B. Johnson Administration.

Further proof of the local chapter's influence in Forum affairs was evidenced when San Angeleños gained several offices in the state organization. Cato Cedillo was picked for first vice chairman, but members of the youth chapter scored the most distinctive victories. Richard V. Garcia, a seventeen-year-old Central High School student, was elected as state chairman of the Junior G.I. Forum, while Olga Ramos gained the vice chairmanship and Ray Moya won the position of treasurer. Additionally, Josie Flores of San Angelo was crowned Queen of the Texas G.I. Forum organization.[23]

Founding the Southside Lions

If Armando Figueroa was politically inclined and business oriented, he was also civic minded. In the late 1950s, Figueroa and some friends decided to affiliate themselves with Lions International, a service association founded in the United States in the 1910s and dedicated to improving the welfare of communities, promoting fellowship, furthering education, and generally improving the common welfare.

According to one explanation of the Mexican Lions Club founding, Figueroa approached members of several Lions organizations in town and asked about joining their club. Eager to further the cause of Lionism, the Anglo Lions responded by creating still one more club in the city, this one composed of men living on the south side. Another version of the club's origins maintains that Anglos did not want Mexican Americans in their all-white clubs. To avoid integration, they sponsored a club composed principally of Mexican Americans.

Whatever the real story, the Southside Lions Club was born in 1959 and chartered on February 16, 1960. P. A. Pichardo, a medical doctor then working for the San Angelo Center, was the first president. Pichardo was followed by other members of the G.I. generation: Armando Figueroa, B. C. Domínguez, Henry V. Vélez, and Ed Idar Jr.

Many members of the Lions Club were defectors from the Senior G.I. Forum. The defections occurred when young members who had belonged to the Junior G.I. Forum pressed for an adult chapter of their own. The older men became unhappy when a charter was granted to the younger group, dissolved the original Forum, and moved to the Southside Lions Club.[24]

Sponsorship of the fiestas patrias was one of the projects undertaken by the new Lions Club. By the early 1960s, the club staged the event at the San Angelo Coliseum, in competition with the aging Sedeño who still held commemoration at his plaza. When Sedeño died in 1974, the Lions assumed full responsibility for backing the fetes, which were held on grounds leased from the city along the South Concho River on the southern outskirts of the town.[25]

The Lions pursued service assignments with much success. The club contributed to the Texas Lions Camp for Crippled Children in Kerrville, Texas, and helped needy children with poor eyesight receive proper care. To this end, the Southside Lions regularly held fundraisers, including benefit dances, menudo cookoffs, and other affairs. Additionally, they held blood drives and supported such programs as donations of organs to eye banks.[26]

High School Seniors

The theory that the Southside Lions Club was created to foster segregation gains some weight in light of an episode that occurred about the same time that the Southside Lions Club was founded. For many years before 1959, Anglo high school seniors had held the "German Dance" to celebrate graduation. The event was held at the country club, a private retreat that catered to the city's elite. As usual, tickets to the dance were being sold that May, and their availability was announced over the loudspeaker at the new Central High School. When the Mexican American students inquired about purchasing them, they were refused on the pretext that it was a private dance and Mexican Americans were not permitted at the country club. Wilma Figueroa, homecoming queen the previous fall, however, had already purchased a ticket and was being escorted by an Anglo boy.

In response, Mr. and Mrs. Máximo Guerrero (parents of a graduate), Armando Figueroa (Wilma's father), and others prepared an alternative dance to honor Mexican American students. The first Mexican American Senior Dance—or Prom—resulted.[27] Held the first year at the Town House Hotel, the dance subsequently moved to the San Angelo Coliseum. By the early 1960s it had taken on the trappings it was known for thereafter:

captured in a beaming spotlight, Mexican American seniors from both Central and Lake View high schools, paraded down the center of the Coliseum floor escorted by their parents, while the master of ceremonies recognized their achievements. Scholarships from Hispanic organizations such as LULAC, the G.I. Forum, or the Southside Lions were granted. A speaker addressed seniors, relatives, and guests. The program was followed by a dance featuring a popular local band.[28]

The major address was delivered by Máximo Guerrero in 1959, and succeeding speakers comprised a veritable Who's Who from San Angelo's Hispanic community. They fall into one of two categories: people who had achieved local prominence, or people who had left the city's barrios to gain distinction elsewhere. The former included Oscar C. Gómez, San Angelo Independent School District board member and board president in the 1980s, and Dick Alcalá, a district attorney during the same period. Among the latter were Noé Camúñez; his sister, Eva Camúñez de Tucker, the first Mexican American to graduate from the city's high school; Mario Castillo, a prominent political appointee in the U.S. Congress; and Mario J. Cruz, a public school counselor in Austin, Texas.

The prom succeeded because, by the 1960s, Mexican Americans in San Angelo were graduating in enough numbers to sustain the annual event. With greater numbers and increased opportunities, Mexican Americans demonstrated excellence in various phases of high school life. Richard Moya, Julio Guerrero, Cecil Salazar, and Charlie Ramírez emerged as sports standouts. Other graduates who made a mark on the local, state, and national level included Oscar C. Gómez, Mario J. Cruz, Mario Castillo, Alberto García, Albert and Andrew Tijerina, and Rosaura Sánchez.

Transition

Like the rest of the United States, the Hispanic

community in San Angelo underwent rapid changes during the 1960s, and these changes challenged the G.I. generation of Mexican American leaders. In some areas these men maintained power. Evelio Villarreal, for instance, was president of the Community Action Council board of directors in 1968.[29] Henry V. Vélez became the director of the Rio Vista Multi-Purpose Center when it opened in 1969.[30] Finally, the G.I. Forum remained firmly in the hands of the older veterans.

At the same time, a new generation of San Angeleños made themselves known. Raised in the chaotic atmosphere of the 1960s and the Viet Nam War, these Mexican Americans questioned decisions of their elders and demanded attention to their problems. Many who first became known during this time assumed leadership roles during the 1970s.

The Viet Nam War was a major influence on these Mexican Americans. Many served in the Armed Forces and, like Daniel Torres and Modesto Gutiérrez, were fortunate to return alive. Others, like Roberto Ríos, Oscar R. Juárez, Mario Gonzales, and Lorenzo Chapa, were killed in action. Albert Tijerina, the first Mexican American drum major at Central High School and a Texas A&M Cadet Corpsman, was killed in Viet Nam in 1971.[31]

Anti-war demonstrations did not develop in San Angelo as they did in other places, but there was opposition from some Mexican Americans. John Chapa, for example, protested the war in a letter to the *Standard-Times* in late October 1969, just a few days after his brother was killed in the conflict.[32]

The black civil rights movement was a second factor causing a transition in the Mexican American community during the 1960s. The struggle of Dr. Martin Luther King and pictures of the attendant violent backlash that came into houses through television moved Mexican Americans, who could hardly fail to identify with a people victimized by prejudice.

Finally, the most important factor promoting change in Mexican American society was the greater number of young Mexican Americans present in the mid-1960s. Products of the post-war baby-boom, this generation was raised in an atmosphere of conflict, protest, and assertion of rights.

In 1967, for example, Mexican Americans from different parts of Texas met in San Antonio and established two organizations intended to capitalize on the growing militancy among Mexican Americans. One organization was the Mexican American Youth Organization (MAYO), which was designed to get Hispanic youths involved in politics. The second was the Raza Unida Party (RUP), which sought to gain political control in those South Texas counties where Mexican Americans made up a majority of the population. José Ángel Gutiérrez, a Texas A & I graduate and resident of Crystal City, Texas, founded both organizations.

Locally, change was detectable in the publication of a series of articles by the city newspaper. During this time, educators, social scientists, and others across the United States took an interest in the Mexican American "sleeping giant," which, according to the logic of the period, was finally awakening after generations of inactivity. Not to be left out, the *Standard-Times* undertook, in June of 1967, a series of eight articles on the status of Mexican Americans in the city.

Nothing this ambitious on the Mexican presence had ever been attempted in San Angelo, and the journalistic investigation was a conspicuous attempt to probe into the "plight" of the Mexican Americans given their "awakening" throughout the Southwest. Reporter David Easterly explained that deplorable living conditions contributed to the rising tide of Hispanic unrest. In San Angelo itself, Easterly found, the south side of the city was a "pocket for poverty stricken people." There, paving was limited to a few main roads, and dusty streets became muddy rivers when it rained. The incidence of Mexican American poverty was higher than the state level, and Texas ranked fifth in poverty among the states in the Southwest. Of the 1,604

Mexican American families in the city counted by the 1960 census, 57.2 percent subsisted on less than $3,000 yearly. Seventy percent of the cases handled by city-county welfare units were Mexican Americans. Moreover, crime was disproportionately high in the barrio. Mexican Americans were involved in more than thirty percent of reported cases of juvenile crime, though Hispanics made up only twenty percent of the city's population. Forty percent of the adults on probation in Tom Green County following felony convictions were Mexican Americans. Housing discrimination was widespread, the reporter noted, thus confining Hispanics to the barrio area.

The situation was considered almost as bad in the schools. Citing a University of California at Los Angeles study that used the late fifties as its base, Easterly noted that, around 1960, San Angelo ranked sixteenth among nineteen metropolitan areas in educational attainment of Mexican Americans. The average grade completed in the city was 4.0 for Mexican Americans compared to 11.5 for Anglos; the UCLA study also determined that in 1950 San Angeleños had an average of 2.9 years of education. Dropout rates were alarming—the 1965 graduating class at Central High included only seventy-five Mexican Americans out of a class of more than 700.

According to Easterly, these figures revealed the "plight" of the Mexican American. Faced by these forces, many San Angeleños developed a "defeatist complex," Easterly learned from interviews of both Anglos and Mexicanos. Victimized by prejudice and accusations of inferiority, youths internalized those attributes and became non-assertive. Furthermore, they found it difficult to learn a foreign language, faced family financial problems, and found it impossible to do good school work while employed as migrant workers.[33]

In his research Easterly apparently failed to realize that defeatism coexisted with increased assertiveness in the Mexican American community. Curiously, the paper originated its ambitious study on local Mexican

American life because Mexican Americans were "restless," yet its reporter found resignation to be the Mexican American lot. In these latter conclusions the *Standard-Times* reflected the accepted wisdom that Mexican Americans were culturally passive and fatalistic. What the newspaper overlooked was an inchoate militancy. But this mistake was understandable, for the newspaper was having to make a judgment during a time of rapid flux.

If the newspaper series pointed to the transitory nature of the times, so did Ed Idar's remarks upon returning in October of that year from the Cabinet Committee Hearings in El Paso. The conference had been part of Lyndon B. Johnson's efforts to deal with the "Mexican problem," and according to Idar, the president was sincerely interested in helping Mexican Americans. "I hope it's not like the case of the Negro people where nothing happened and they grew desperate and resorted to tactics not sensible," asserted Idar. Those who Idar feared might become "desperate" were the young Mexican Americans who held a rival conference in El Paso at the same time.[34] Militants at the El Paso meeting denounced the Johnson hearings as a fraud and an effort to appease rather than satisfy Hispanics who were demanding an equal share of the American dream.

By the mid-1960s, two movements existed side by side among Mexican Americans. In San Angelo, the split was reflected by the presence of one group consisting of men of World War II vintage who still occupied posts in government bodies and asserted leadership roles[35] and a group of younger Mexican Americans from the high school and Angelo State University who were led by peers or by older Hispanics who sensed the tenor of the times and adjusted their ideology accordingly.

CHAPTER SEVEN

Chicano Years, 1969-1974

The attitudes of San Angeleños in the late 1960s reflected events occurring throughout Texas, particularly in the southern part of the state. During the era, Mexican American youths enrolled in colleges and universities in record numbers, many with financial assistance from Great Society programs. On campus, many Mexican Americans became involved in the debate over Viet Nam and America's treatment of ethnic minorities.

These issues helped create a new consciousness among Mexican American college students. At the same time, there was a rising militancy among Mexican Americans in the poorest classes. This particularly was shown in efforts to organize farm workers in the Rio Grande Valley. In 1966, South Texas *campesinos* (farm workers) organized a march to Austin to emphasize their plight. Old activists from the G.I. generation—Hector P. García, for example—joined the march. For many college students, the march was a reminder of their origins and their common relationship with field hands. As a result, Mexican Americans organized committees at the University of Texas at Austin and other colleges to support the farm workers' unionizing efforts. The Mexican American Student Organization (MAYO) and the Raza Unida Party (RUP) were born out of this enthusiasm.

The same spirit which gave birth to MAYO and RUP fixed upon the word "Chicano" as a political symbol. The word, according to Professor José Limón, "became an ideological term, designating individuals [of Hispanic origin] who were promoting an intense ethnic nationalism that would lead to a vaguely defined political and cultural liberation of the 'Chicano' community."[1]

Old conditions of poverty and persistent feelings of oppression were at the root of Chicano protest in the late 1960s. Such problems were not absent in San Angelo, which by 1970 was a city with 12,500 Spanish surnamed citizens. According to a Tom Green County Community Action Council (TGC-CAC) report released in August 1969, the 3,000 people living in Census Tract 14 (see map) had a median income of $2,400 a year, and the median school years completed was about four. Twenty-five percent of the population earned $2,000 or less per annum. In Census Tract 9, the median income for the 2,000 inhabitants was $3,218, and the median school years completed was about eight.[2] Tracts 9 and 14 had the highest concentrations of Mexican Americans in the city. In Tract 9, 63.8 percent of the population was Spanish surnamed, and in Tract 14, 93.6 percent of the people had Spanish surnames. Residents in the two tracts worked in a variety of jobs across the city, but they were heavily engaged as laborers, operatives (seamstresses, butchers, welders, etc.), and private household workers. The area south of Avenue N had the least expensive houses in the city.[3]

Like Mexican Americans through the state, San Angeleños wanted to improve their economic conditions. In 1967, Maria Cardenas, a resident of the south side wrote a letter to the *Standard-Times* expressing her view on the farm workers' unionization efforts in the Lower Rio Grande Valley. To her, unions would not have been necessary if Mexicanos had not been worked "half to death on starvation wages." Given their plight, she noted, no wonder they sought to better their future through collective bargaining.[4]

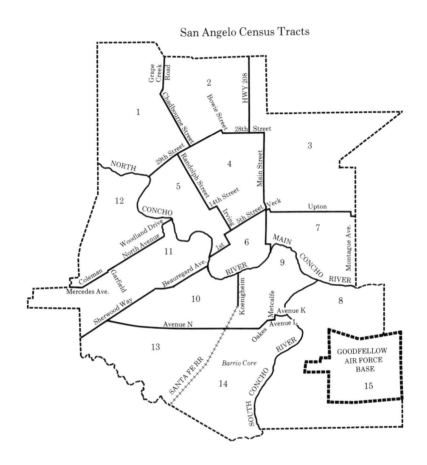

San Angelo Census Tracts

In October of 1969, another letter appeared in the *Standard-Times* that unveiled a smoldering anxiety among younger Mexican Americans about the older generation. Written by Angelo State University student Nemesio Pérez Jr., it noted that parents were economically obligated to Anglos and so were limited in the ways they could help the Mexican American people. Mexican adults, Pérez noted, had done little historically, and "it is our duty to help fellow Chicanos educate themselves. The problem of youth is that the adults are not trying to help us."[5] In truth, young Pérez' emphasis on improving conditions was one that each generation had embraced. By the late 1960s, however, Pérez' impatient generation wanted to offer new tactics.

The 1970 City Election

By the late 1960s, the Chicano movement in South Texas had reached San Angelo, and increased political activity resulted. Between 1970 and 1974, more than ten Mexican Americans ran for city or county positions. Of these, three were middle-aged and had fought in World War II; the formative years for the rest had been the 1950s and the 1960s. All were inspired by the atmosphere of assertiveness and the belief Mexican Americans could triumph in a changing climate.

To further the cause, Nemesio Pérez and others organized the Chicano Student Organization at Angelo State University in 1969.[6] In December of that year, Pérez and fellow collegians Elías and Sylvia Lara went to Crystal City, Texas, to instruct high school students then boycotting classes in protest of educational discrimination.[7] After these experiences, and after helping in a voter registration drive early in 1970, Pérez decided to run for Place 6 in the city commission election that March.

The election also attracted Mexican American moderates, like Isaac Olivares Jr., who ran for Place 3. Olivares was a graduate of ASU and worked as treasurer of the First Savings and Loan Association. He said he entererd the race because he was concerned over the city's handling of revenues. In ethnic politics, he noted Mexican American representation was essential if the political troubles experienced by other West Texas cities were to be avoided. Pérez, twenty-one years old, argued that Mexican Americans needed representation in the city commission since no communication existed between municipal government and the barrio. He promised to work for a better sewer system, new street lighting, construction of overpasses by schools, and a park in South San Angelo.[8]

In the election, Pérez lost but Olivares gained a place in the runoff. In April, Olivares defeated his opponent, thus becoming the first Mexican American in four years to serve on the city commission.[9]

Protest at Precinct 14

The "Chicano Movement" in San Angelo was further manifest in an incident involving an election judge in the Precinct 14 ballot box at Rio Vista Elementary School. During the June 6 Democratic Primary runoff election, some forty Mexican Americans held a peaceful demonstration at the school grounds in an attempt to persuade voters to boycott the election. Marchers paraded in front of Rio Vista holding signs saying *"no voten,"* "Down with White, Up with Brown," and "We've Waited Long Enough." Efforts by local Democratic party leaders to stop the demonstration only provoked shouts from the marchers that they were a different breed of Mexican Americans not cowed or appeased like the older generation. According to Frank Dominguez, one of the protesters, the issue at hand was the unwillingness of Anglos to have Mexican Americans choose their own election judge; instead a judge from another precinct supervised the election. Rebecca Aguirre, appointed to work at the election, resigned her position and joined the marchers when, allegedly, she was told she could not work at the front table but had to count ballots in the back. Nemesio Pérez, another protester, declared that the demonstration was part of a struggle to wrest control from Anglos. Only about eight percent of the registered voters for the Río Vista precinct cast ballots that day.[10]

The boycott did not change the minds of the Tom Green County Commissioners. On July 17 they had to replace the Anglo election judge, who had resigned following the June boycott. Disregarding requests from both the County Republican Chairman and fifteen Mexican Americans proposing that either Rebecca Aguirre, Richard Esquivel, or Armando Treviño (Republican) be appointed election judge for Precinct 14, the commissioners appointed another Anglo.[11]

A spate of letters to the *Standard-Times* followed. The letters came from different quarters but expressed the same theme—the demands of the barrio were justified. Father Larry Underdonk of St. Mary's Church and the Reverend Juan Salinas of Bethel Methodist Church (115 W. Avenue O), both of whom had supported the boycott, noted that the displeasure in the barrio was understandable considering the continued perceptions of oppression. When an Anglo responded that Salinas was evidently representing a "bunch of Mexican people" who refused to learn English, another rash of letters to the editor followed. One of them came from the G.I. Forum, and it reminded the Anglo writer that ancestors of Mexican Americans had settled in the Southwest before Englishmen populated the Atlantic coast. "The United States came to us," it asserted, "if there is a foreign language here, surely it is the English language."[12] Thus, even the older established groups were in accord with the younger generation's sentiments, though not necessarily sharing its tactics.

The Precinct 14 protesters met at the Río Vista Center on August 3 to plan their next move. At the meeting, they decided to circulate a petition calling for the revocation of the Anglo judge's appointment and the assignment of a Mexican American to the post. Heated exchanges, between Frank Domínguez and Nemesio Pérez on one side and the Tom Green County

Democratic Party leadership and the newly appointed Anglo election judge on the other, electrified the meeting. The Chicano leaders demanded the judge's resignation, arguing that the voters did not want him. The judge argued that he had been legally appointed by the commissioners. The meeting ended amid threats of an economic boycott.[13]

A compromise was reached four days later. Frank Domínguez was appointed precinct chairman for the barrio and several qualified Hispanic voters were to help with the general election that November. The election judge appointed by the commissioners in July kept his post.[14] Then, less than two weeks before the election, the Anglo judge fell sick. Richard Esquivel, a General Telephone employee, was named temporary election judge of Precinct 14 in Río Vista School.[15] With the appointment of Domínguez, both parties had a Mexican American precinct chairman at Precinct 14. Armando Treviño served in that capacity for the Republicans.

The 1971 Election

Evelio Villarreal, the Forumeer, entered the school board race in February 1971. Villarreal was a former president of the Tom Green County Community Action Council, a member of the Southside Lions Club, American Legion, G.I. Forum, Boys Club, and YMCA. He promised his efforts would be directed toward helping all the people, not just Mexican Americans.[16] Although Villarreal would have made a strong candidate, he soon learned he was disqualified for office because a relative worked as a teacher in the school system. Villarreal withdrew in favor of Sabino Garcia, a production supervisor at Ethicon, Inc. Caught on short notice, Garcia's campaign never gained momentum; another candidate won.[17]

Chicanos

Though the Chicano Movement was manifest in San

Angelo by 1969, Mexican Americans in the city did not organize chapters of MAYO for another two years. In September 1971, students from Angelo State University and Central High School held an organizational meeting in order to affiliate with the statewide group. According to Gerardo (Jerry) Pérez, one of the organizers, the local body intended to focus on worthwhile projects in the Mexican American neighborhoods—among them cleaning up the barrio, founding a community store, and getting a meeting place for youths. They also planned to help Mexican Americans with employment and educational opportunities.[18]

Bringing unity to the Mexican American community was another important goal of MAYO members. They envisioned a council of "Chicano oriented organizations" and "concerned individuals" that would facilitate dialogue between their youth corps and other Hispanic groups that did not share their militant stand yet believed in the common goal of bettering Mexican American conditions. To initiate such ambitions, MAYO leaders hosted a gathering at La Academia on Knickerbocker Road in late November. Among those attending were representatives of the Mexican American Association at Central High, Alumnos de Amistad from Lake View High School, and the Chicano Student Organization at Angelo State University. Interested persons from the Southside Lions, the G.I. Forum Ladies Auxiliary, and a newly formed group of older Mexican Americans called the Consejo del Barrio (Council of the Barrio) also were present, but strictly in the capacity of interested people, not as representatives of their particular clubs. Much of the discussion on the need for unity was done by Jerry Pérez, Nemesio Pérez, and Carlos Aguilar, and it was agreed, mostly by the younger representatives from the three schools, that future meetings would be fruitful.[19] The proposed council, however, apparently did not materialize.

MAYO members also worked for social betterment by allying themselves with the RUP, which offered itself as an alternative to the Democratic and Republican parties in Texas. When RUP held its state meeting in San Antonio in November 1971, those attending included Jerry Pérez, Carlos Aguilar, and María Cardenas. Billy G. Torres, an Angelo State University student, was seated on the platform committee.[20]

A non-MAYO organization appeared in 1971 under the name of the Consejo del Barrio. This was made up of older members of the south barrio, and according to the Reverend Juan Salinas, the chairman, the group lacked formal structure. Its purpose was to listen to problems of local residents, then take action. Elaborating further, vice chairperson María Cardenas said that the group's objectives included getting parents and barrio residents involved in solving problems. In 1971, cases of mistreatment in the schools, discrimination, and traffic ticket problems were among the Consejo's major concerns.[21] The Consejo's connection to Chicano-oriented groups in the city had much to do with María Cardenas' presence in both. Cardenas had the singular ability to make herself acceptable to both old and young.

Raza Unida—1972

Heightened interest in city and county politics continued in 1972. Running for the school board that year was Ernest Pérez, a contract estimator with Terrill Manufacturing Company. "I have always been interested in education and I would be a person to serve the people of San Angelo on a fair and impartial basis," said Pérez.[22] Isaac Olivares ran for reelection to the City Commission, but his race was dimmed by an alleged feud he was having with the Chief of Police.[23] Joining the race for another City Commission spot was Billy G. Torres, the MAYO chairman and RUP delegate.[24] All three lost.[25]

Politics for the year were not over, however, for RUP was running a candidate for governor, and San Angelo MAYO members and others were eager to participate in an election featuring Richard M. Nixon and George McGovern at the national level. After a visit to the city by Ramsey Muñiz, the RUP gubernatorial candidate, temporary county RUP chairman Jerry Pérez announced that the local chapter of Raza Unida would hold precinct conventions in private homes.[26]

In August, both Muñiz and his running mate, Alma Canales, visited San Angelo to rally support for Raza Unida.[27]

In September, María Cardenas of Consejo del Barrio, her son Abel Cardenas, and Billy G. Torres, attended the RUP national convention in El Paso. Mrs. Cardenas was seated as a voting delegate and Torres as an alternate.[28]

As the November election approached, Mexican Americans faced several choices on how to serve their interests. To Isaac Olivares, the ex-city commissioner supporting the Republican Party, Muñiz was a tantalizing alternative, and, despite his steadfast support for other Republican candidates, Olivares declared that Mexican Americans should vote for the RUP gubernatorial candidate. Mrs. Frank (María) Domínguez, a staunch Democrat, agreed with the idea of supporting Muñiz; otherwise, she felt Mexican Americans should vote Democrat. María Cardenas was the most strident RUP supporter.[29] In the election, a Republican won the presidency, a Democrat won the governorship, and the RUP won only scattered victories in South Texas.

Cato Cedillo

Political fervor spilled over into 1973 as three more Mexican Americans offered themselves to the voters. Abel Cardenas Jr., the eighteen-year-old son of María Cardenas and a Raza Unida supporter, declared his intention to run for Place 5 in the city commission because representation was needed for the "Chicano community." If elected, Abel promised to work to establish a free health clinic for the needy and to reduce city bus rates. More ambitiously, Abel proposed the creation of single-member districts, which had been legitimized in the case of *Regester* v. *White* in early 1973.[30]

Also delving into politics for the first time was Cato Cedillo, G.I. Forumeer, long-standing resident of the south barrio and golf course superintendent. Cedillo wanted the city to maintain youth programs threatened by phase-outs in Washington.[31] Ernest Pérez ran again for the school board on a platform of "community wide" representation and improving the quality of education.[32] Only Cedillo won election.[33]

The Older Generation Gives Politics a Try—1974

With the exception of Evelio Villarreal, all who sought election during this time were part of the postwar era; some were born during the Korean conflict. But in 1974, two World War II veterans, who had long been active in civic matters and had been in the forefront of Hispanic matters in the 1950s and 1960s, finally gave politics a try.

B. C. Domínguez, an experienced police officer with more than twenty years in law enforcement, ran for police chief. Domínguez promised to improve supervision, strengthen the chain of command, improve working conditions, enhance the image of policemen, and find money for officer education programs.[34]

Businessman and civic leader Henry V. Vélez, sought a place on the County Commission, making him the second Hispanic to seek that office since the days of Pablo Alderette. Vélez' credentials included his work with the Southside Lions Club, Community Chest Drive, G.I. Forum, and LULAC. If elected, Vélez promised to identify the needs of poor people and initiate ways to alleviate their distress.[35]

The two Mexican American candidates ran effective campaigns, but both lost in runoffs: Domínguez by 256 votes; Vélez by 171.[36]

The defeats of Domínguez and Vélez signaled the loss

of ground for the "G.I. generation" in San Angelo. Events had changed too quickly in the late 1960s and early 1970s. Mexican Americans who came of political age during this period, however, often lost sight of the gains made by the war generation and accused them of having "done little for Mexicanos." In spite of this attitude, the youths were willing to vote for a member of the G.I. generation when the alternative was someone from the outside or who represented a philosophy unsympathetic to Mexican American needs.

Decline of the New and the Old

The Chicano movement represented by MAYO and RUP was on the wane by 1974. The end of the VietNam War left many without a cause, and the youths of the 1960s passed into an age group where raising families, and paying for houses and cars, took primacy over political activities.

So, while Chicano militancy had been in vogue for several years, it seemed passé by the mid-1970s. RUP supporters had trouble putting together a campaign staff for the gubernatorial race of 1974,[37] and visits by Muñiz—again the candidate—touched only the committed. Muñiz' defeat by a wider margin than in 1972 took its toll on those evaluating the future of a third party.

In subsequent years, the militant rhetoric of the past era still echoed from the young who had participated in the tail-end of the movement. Denunciations of white society were expressed at Angelo State University and in "Viewpoints" printed in the *Standard-Times*.[38] Others questioned the meaning of the United States Bicentennial in 1976. But as the seventies progressed, such voices were heard less often and the country moved into a more conservative age.

If militancy was on the decline by the late 1970s, so was the role of older spokespersons like those of the G.I. Forum. Since the establishment of a chapter in San Angelo in 1948, the G.I. Forum had worked diligently for Mexican Americans in the city and, throughout the "Chicano era," had continued as the moderate voice of the Hispanic community. Though the organization avoided the Precinct 14 flap and MAYO and RUP, it supported voter registration drives, supported Hispanic election judges, looked into cases of police brutality against Mexican Americans, and assisted in the campaigns of Villarreal, Cedillo, Domínguez, and Vélez. But, by the mid-1970s, Forumeers had reached middle age. Many of their old causes were no longer problems. Poll taxes were unconstitutional, street paving programs were under way, and fedral agencies supplanted the role of old G.I. Forum self-help projects.[39]

After the mid-1970s, the G.I. Forum in San Angelo became low-keyed. In October 1975, it sponsored an immensely successful banquet for Dr. Hector P. Garcia, the Forum's founder, and the occasion afforded the leadership—Willie Serna Sr., Joe Gonzales, and Pete Chapa—the chance to invite state politicians to present their political platform before the public. Among those attending was the Texas Secretary of State, Mark White.[40] In later years, the local Forum resurrected sports banquets like the ones of the 1960s to inspire, as president Cato Cedillo put it, the "Julio Guerreros" to continue with their high school athletic careers instead of being pushed out at the junior high level.[41]

The decline of the G.I. Forum was due to the changing of the times, not a result of declining interest in self-betterment among Mexican Americans. Once again, a new organization emerged—or, more exactly, an old group was revived. After being supplanted by the G.I. Forum in the 1950s, the LULAC was reborn to serve the needs of both the youth of the 1960s and the G.I. generation of the 1940s and 1950s.

CHAPTER EIGHT

Towards Equality, 1975-1984

In its rejuvenated form, LULAC emerged in the 1970s as the organization to voice Mexican American aspirations. San Angelo Council 152 had died in the early fifties, but a score of years later a Chicano leadership with new sets of approaches was evolving to assume the goals of previous generations. LULAC, founded in Corpus Christi in 1929, had suffered from several problems since World War II. Forumeers said LULAC was too riddled with factionalism; Chicano activitists said LULAC was too gradualist and assimilationist. By the mid-1970s, however, LULAC had built a reputation for being able to use conventional means to achieve its ends.

Isaac Olivares, the ex-city commissioner, realized the need for a new LULAC chapter in 1972. After discussing the prospects with interested Mexican Americans that October, he drafted a letter and mailed it to several people active in community affairs. It invited them to an organizational meeting at the old Mexican Grill, where an attempt would be made to found a chapter of LULAC.[1]

In May 1973, the efforts of Olivares and his colleagues paid off when Texas State Director Tony Bonilla came to San Angelo and presented a charter founding Council 637. Tommy Robles was elected president; other officers and members included Marcus Balderas, Nellie Galindo, Mr. and Mrs. Frank Domínguez, and Pete Chapa. All worked in some professional or semi-professional capacity; indeed, leadership in the 1970s and 1980s generally derived from the middle class, politically moderate, and college educated segment of San Angelo's Hispanic society. The members envisioned the council as an instrument dedicated to bettering conditions for the Mexican American community in San Angelo. Problems in education, civil rights, housing, job training and placement would be investigated and resolved by working through the bureaucratic structure with which most were well acquainted.[2]

To bring about educational improvement, LULAC worked through several avenues. By tapping the generosity of local philanthropists and organizations and holding fund-raising banquets, it collected scholarship funds and dispersed them to worthy Mexican American college students.[3] Additionally, the local council sponsored educational seminars,[4] supported bilingual education,[5] and assisted the campaign of sympathetic school board candidates.

LULAC also was interested in improving conditions for Mexican Americans in the San Angelo schools. In February 1983, the council responded to pleas from students at John Glenn Junior High School (opened in 1967 at 2201 University Avenue) who alleged unfair treatment following a scrap between a group of Mexican Americans and junior high athletes (including both Anglos and Hispanics). Subsequent to the incident, the Mexican American youths were taken to jail by the police, where they were interviewed, then released, while the athletes were permitted to go home with their parents. With help from the national LULAC organization and led by Berta Pérez Linton, a sister of Nemesio Pérez, the Chicano Student Organization leader of the early 1970s, Council 637 called on the Education Department of the federal Civil Rights Office to investigate the San Angelo Independent School District for possible discrimination against

Hispanics. LULAC alleged that Hispanic students were treated differently from the predominantly Anglo group involved in the scuffle. Moreover, the council complained that the school district discriminated in hiring Mexican American teachers and administrators.

In July 1983, the U.S. Department of Education Office of Civil Rights ruled that Hispanics had received different treatment following the February skirmish. On the other hand, the same report cleared the San Angelo public schools of discrimination in hiring practices. To avert further trouble, the school board made changes in the Glenn administration. Additional Mexican American teachers were hired by the beginning of the 1983-1984 school year.[6]

LULAC Council 637 also tried opening opportunities for the economically disadvantaged, underemployed, and unemployed. In 1974-1975, it attempted to establish the federally funded Service, Employment, and Redevelopment (SER) program. Spearheaded by San Angelo attorney Louis Pérez, SER entailed providing on-the-job training for individuals below the poverty line. Employers in the Tom Green County area would train SER people and then provide them with jobs. The Concho Valley Council of Governments (CVCOG) office would be responsible for funding the program. Differences surfaced between LULAC and CVCOG, however, and the implementation of the project was halted in March 1975.[7]

In a move to assist Mexican American businessmen in the city, LULACers in 1976 and 1977 sponsored a program named the Volunteer Committee for the Promotion of Business (VCPB). Funded by the U.S. Department of Commerce, VCPB was designed to distribute business operations information and act as a liaison between potential and existing businessmen and lending institutions and creditor agencies. Further, the VCPB office was to coordinate assistance and provide training and technical help to existing or potential business people.[8] This LULAC project expired after it exhausted its initial funding from the federal government. By then, it had fulfilled its purpose.[9]

LULACers also sought to insure that local poverty agencies effectively served the Mexican American poor. Within months after its founding, Council 637 demanded a position on the Community Action Council (CAC) board of directors and subsequently worked closely with the CAC to see that the impoverished and disadvantaged were properly tended to.[10] The council also moved to see that there were Hispanics appointed to policy-making boards, including the City Planning Commission and the Citizens Utility Rate Board (CURB). Council 637's legal counsel Berta Pérez Linton went before the City Council in January 1983 and threatened legal action if the council did not allow room for Hispanics on CURB. The city body defended itself by maintaining that the absence of Mexican Americans from the board was not a result of discrimination but an oversight by the city council.[11]

Though a non-political organization, LULAC also used the voice and strength that it got from the national office to preserve the political rights of Mexican Americans. In 1978, for example, a LULAC rally before the Tom Green County courthouse protested a wave of police brutality across the state.[12] In December 1981, LULAC president Willie Serna Sr., supported by the local chapter of the American G.I. Forum[13] and interested black organizations, initiated a suit against the Tom Green County Commissioners, challenging their redistricting plan. According to the plantiffs, the commissioners' apportionment design, which raised the minority population of Precinct 2 to forty-five percent, diluted minority strength, fragmented the minority population, violated their constitutional rights, and intentionally discriminated against minorities. Roberto Soto, a native San Angeloan working for West Texas Legal Services and representing the aggrieved parties, pressed for fifty-eight percent Hispanic and black representation in a class action suit filed in federal court. In late January 1982, Soto, LULAC and its allies accepted a plan offered by Tom Green County attorneys which created sixty-two percent minority population in Precinct 1.[14]

LULAC also responded to job discrimination complaints. Such a case in 1978 led to a threat to file suit against Angelo State University for being lax in pursuing affirmative action. Intervention by the Health, Education, and Welfare office in Dallas led to an amicable agreement between the council and Angelo State.[15]

Numerous other problems brought Council 637 into San Angelo and state affairs. These included efforts to correct stereotypes perpetuated by the media, to represent minority interests on particular issues, to obtain better pay for farm workers, and to protect the rights of undocumented immigrants from Mexico.

Conventional Politics

In 1975, Oscar C. Gómez captured a place on the San Angelo Independent School District school board. Gómez graduated from Central High School in 1964 and earned his degree at Angelo State University. As a teacher in one of the local junior high schools in the latter part of the decade, he avoided the controversial aspects of the Chicano movement, then left to earn a master's degree at Arizona State University. After a time as a counselor at Central High, he had turned to the business world and worked for General Telephone in the revenue and earnings department when he was elected to the school board.[16]

Gómez' victory signaled a new trend among Mexican American politicians. Those who sought political office after 1975 usually were college educated and thus had the necessary credentials that "qualified" them to represent all San Angeloans. In general, Hispanic political aspirants before this time were not university trained and therefore lacked credibility among Anglos. The post-1975 generation of politicians resembled the LULACers in the sense that they were in professional occupations, but they were different from members of

Council 637 in that they did not take the public "pro-Mexicano" stance that the LULACers did. Nonetheless, the groups were closely tied. Gómez' workers, for example, included several LULACers, among them Louis Pérez and Tommy Robles, and it was they who in 1975 skillfully managed a "vote just for Oscar" campaign rather than for the three trustee choices in the city-wide race.[17]

Despite the greater willingness of Anglos to accept Mexican Americans into the larger society, the college educated candidates who ran after 1975 were unable to form the necessary coalition to win office. Many Anglos remained reluctant to vote for Mexican Americans, and an Hispanic candidate usually carried the Mexican American boxes but lost elsewhere. Alex Tafolla failed in his bid for the City Commission in 1977;[18] others defeated during this time included Johnny Benavides for Chief of Police (1980), Ralph Villarreal (1980)[19] and Berta Pérez Linton (1981) for the School Board,[20] Al Celaya for County Clerk (1982),[21] Ray O. Hernández for State Representative (1982),[22] and Daniel Móntez for the City Commission (1983).[23] The best possibilities for winning office were in those areas of the city where Mexican Americans made up a substanial part of the constituency.

Two people—exceptions to the rule of the "educated, middle-class, professional" candidates—did win in the 1970s. Cato Cedillo was able to capitalize on his city-wide reputation to win reelection in 1975; in 1977 he was mayor pro-tem.[24] Although Cedillo was not a college graduate, his campaign was managed by educated, middle-class professionals in the Mexican American community.

Once in office, Cedillo exerted enough political clout to carry out several long-term projects. His work on a street improvement program reduced the number of unpaved streets in the barrio from twenty-five to ten between 1973-1978. Two recreation centers, one built in South Angelo on Ben Ficklin Road, received Cedillo's staunch support. Also, an improved city hiring policy that did not discriminate against minorities was finalized during Cedillo's years in office.[25]

Maria Cardenas was a unique case. Cardenas was veteran of grassroots work and the Raza Unida Party of the Chicano era. By 1975, she had enrolled at Angelo State University, recognizing her lack of education to be a liability in the quest for political office; she graduated in 1983.

Cardenas' strengths included a canny political nose and an image in the barrio as a common person able to articulate the needs of the lower class. Her first major plunge into city-wide politics came in 1976 when she spearheaded the effort to achieve a change to the single-member district system. At the time, all seven council members, including the mayor, ran at-large. Cardenas and other single-member district supporters succeeded in forcing the issue onto the 1976 ballot, where it was approved by a wide margin.[26]

In the first single-member district election in 1978, Cardenas ran for the City Commission District 3 and defeated her two opponents. Her district included the predominantly Mexican American section of town,[27] and she carefully cultivated her image as "one of the barrio." Dressing simply and talking directly, Cardenas accomplished most of her goals by a technique that involved shrewdness, brashness, and intimidation of foes with charges of racism.

With her solid political base in the barrio, Cardenas could consciously depart from the image of the middle class Mexican American who sought to represent all the people; as her strength on the City Commission increased, she could reject that role altogether. In 1980, Cardenas ran without opposition, and in a survey taken that summer to determine the most powerful people in San Angelo, Cardenas was the only woman ranked among the top twenty-five.[28] Cardenas was reelected in 1982[29] and subsequently selected as mayor pro-tem for 1982-1983.[30]

In 1984, Cardenas ran for the Precinct 1 position on the County Commission, but her strengths in the predominantly Mexican American section of town turned into liabilities in a situation where her candidacy had to be broadened to incorporate new areas. Her independence, her image as a "barrio person," her identification with "Mexican causes," her abrasive techniques in getting things done did not win new constituents. Cardenas' old style of barrio politics—which involved door-to-door canvassing, an improvised election staff comprised primarily of her family, plus a low campaign budget—proved ineffective. Instead, the Democratic nomination went to sixty-two-year-old retired policeman B. C. Domínguez, who resurfaced from the politics of the early seventies and was shrewdly presented by the new generation of middle-class professionals on his campaign staff as a non-controversial candidate for all the people.[31]

Successes and Failures

For a large portion of Mexican Americans in the 1980s, life in San Angelo was comfortable and beneficial. Many could afford homes in the better residential additions; some lived in the affluent west part of town. There were professionals of every kind, among them District Attorney Dick Alcalá[32] and private lawyers like Louis Pérez, Berta Pérez Linton, and Joe Hernández. Al Celaya was Elections Administrator for Tom Green County, Raymond Holguín was Chief of the Adult Probation Office, Alex Tafolla was Community Development and Housing Director for San Angelo, and J. D. Córtez was Executive Director of the Community Action Council. Politicians included Oscar C. Gómez as president of the School Board and Danny Cardenas as City Commissioner.

In education, Mexican Americans were present in practically every aspect of the profession. Santos Elizondo became principal of Río Vista in 1972, and Mexicanos were chosen subsequently for similar posts in other elementary schools.[33] Hispanics also taught throughout the district. Furthermore, students mingled freely with Anglo and black classmates, especially beyond the elementary level, and won honors frequently in academic and sports-related areas. In high school, the number of students more closely approximated the general proportion of Mexican Americans in San Angelo; about twenty-five percent of the 1984 graduates had Spanish surnames.[34] At Angelo State University, Mexican American professors first arrived in 1973. Manuel Luján became registrar in 1978.

The business sector included a share of very successful entrepreneurs. Ricardo Fuentes and Henry Hogeda owned thriving restaurants, Jesse Zapata ran a prosperous insulation company, and Nick García financed a shopping center next to the barrio.[35] In the summer of 1977, a common interest brought these and other Hispanic businessmen together to form the Concho Valley Chamber of Commerce (CVCC). An offshoot of the LULAC-sponsored VCPB, the CVCC sought to promote the goals of its predominantly Mexican American membership, sponsored seminars on better business methods, and served as a forum for the exchange of ideas.[36] By the early 1980s, however, the organization floundered and soon died.

Careers in the media, real estate, law enforcement, probation, social work, and the postal service—Lonnie Monreal was postmaster in San Angelo—also lured Mexican Americans.[37] Further, San Angelo was home for Lorenzo Castañeda, a well-known painter of western scenes, and Tony Guerrero, acknowledged for his contribution to Chicano music.

Service organizations lived on. In 1985, the Southside Lions Club would celebrate twenty-five years of existence. With a new generation of members in its ranks—many of them college educated—the club pressed strongly forward. A Lioness Club, founded in 1982, furthered the cause of Lionism. Another women's society, Las Tejanas, provided scholarships for Mexican American girls pursuing academic careers. Scholarships usually were granted at the Mexican American Senior Dance in May.[38]

But while many San Angeleños owned a share of the American dream, not everyone enjoyed that blessing. About one-fourth of Mexicanos in San Angelo still lived in poor conditions in the enclave extending south from the North Concho River. La Loma remained the barrio core,[39] even though streets now were paved and sanitary facilities were on a par with those in other areas of the city. The mean income for Hispanic families, according to the 1980 census, was about $14,000 per year compared to the city's overall income of slightly more than $21,000 per family.[40]

Besides María Cardenas, two other leaders worked to improve conditions in the barrio. One of them, María Talamantes, claimed a record of accomplishments that went back to the years of the Chicano Movement, when she toiled alongside her activist husband, Frank Domínguez, who died in 1974. Talamantes was a grassroots worker in civic activities ranging from Planned Parenthood of San Angelo through election judge for Precinct 14, to president of the Río Vista Head Start Program. She also was instrumental in the development of a sidewalk to John Glenn Junior High School, the building of an overhead crossing for Bryant Boulevard, the reduction of bus rates for school children and the elderly, the securing of housing for the needy and meals for the elderly, and the printing of bilingual election ballots.[41] Furthermore, Talamantes played a large part in the selection of park sites for the barrio, one of which was named "Pete Chapa Park" after the long-time G.I. Forumeer and civic activist.[42]

The Reverend Tomás Chávez, who arrived in San Angelo in 1974, attended to the poor by using the concept of "Serv-Iglesia" (servant church). Through Proyecto Dignidad, his Nazareth Presbyterian Church, headquartered at 313 West Avenue N, Chávez distributed groceries, provided volunteer day care, offered counsel and medical assistance, and carried out programs for senior citizens. The pastoral care was financed through donations from other churches, sale of tamales, car washes, and similar activities. Clients were expected to compensate the church with their labor.[43]

San Angeleños continued to encounter racism in the 1980s, although seldom in its blatant and virulent form. Racism now was manifest in ethnic jokes and epithets and in subtle actions taken by landlords, employers, municipal officials, and voters. Bolder racists wrote letters to the *Standard-Times* expressing their dislike for "Mexicans."

Although some battles in education had been won, others remained. Mexican Americans made up about thirty-three percent of the San Angelo Independent School District enrollment, yet only 8.5 percent of the teachers and six percent of the administrators were Hispanics in 1983.[44]

In some of the predominantly Mexican American schools, according to some stories, teachers taunted Hispanic students with pejorative labels of "wetbacks" and encouraged them to go "cook their beans" and drop out of school since they would not amount to much in society anyway.[45] At Edison Junior High School, two Mexican American teachers in 1984 were coldly ostracized by some of their colleagues for siding with a Hispanic student who implicated one of her teachers in a child molestation case.[46]

A Final Look

The census of 1980 put the number of Hispanics in San Angelo at 16,828.[47] This was a heterogeneous population which ranged from recent arrivals from Mexico to those completely assimilated to American norms and almost completely Anglicized. Overall, however, most San Angeleños were bicultural. They spoke English, dressed in American fashions, enjoyed mainstream American music, and followed many of Anglo society's tenets. Some Hispanics even projected the "redneck" image found in the Southern states and West Texas.

In spite of this, loyalty to Mexican heritage was commonplace. The Spanish language in San Angelo, for instance, was very much part of Mexican American life, especially in the barrios. A Spanish-language radio station served the area until 1983, when its format was changed to country western music, which generated more money according to the station manager. Many Spanish-speaking listeners protested the change.[48] Political advertisements and ballots still had to be printed in a bilingual format in the barrio. Many barrio children attended the first grade as Spanish mono-linguals, but bilingual education eased their transition into an English curriculum. At the same time many San Angeleños consciously cultivated their Spanish, and undocumented workers who became part of barrio society further nurtured the language.

Stores that catered to Mexican American tastes in food were found in the city, especially in the places close to the barrio. *Panaderías* (bakeries), *tortillerías* (tortilla factories), and *tendajos* (small grocery stores) selling items and ingredients that were part of Mexican foods were integral to Mexican American neighborhoods. Some of the latter produced traditional foods like *barbacoa mexicana* (Mexican barbecue), tamales, and cabrito (kid). On Sunday mornings, Mexican Americans from different parts of the city journeyed to barrio stores to get pots of menudo, the tripe dish regarded by *La Raza* as the "breakfast of champions."

Mexican music also was popular in the city. Until its aforementioned demise in 1983, Spanish-language station KSJT kept lively tunes going, and Hispanic appreciation for it was manifest in the existence of Mexican music stores and the sale of Spanish records in Anglo record shops.

Weekend dances held throughout the city by local impresarios were another reflection of love for Mexican American music. Major Chicano bands traveled to San Angelo to play before large crowds; many events sold out the city coliseum. Other ballrooms, such as Carlos Martinez' El Cielito Lindo, on the old Ballinger Highway, hosted full houses every week.

Traditional events such as weddings, graduations, and *quinceañeras* (fifteenth birthday parties) were also occasions for dances. Quinceañeras were significant episodes in Mexican American girls' lives, for they commemorated a girl's passage from adolescence to womanhood. Rooted in Aztec and Mayan customs, the occasion incorporated religious solemnity with the social ambience of a fiesta. The celebration started with the quinceañera—a fifteen-year-old-girl—escorted by *padrinos* ("sponsors or godparents"), going to church and having the priest or minister bless her coming of age. A dinner then followed. That evening, padrinos sponsoring the quinceañera promenaded to *la marcha* and danced to the music of popular local bands such as Roberto Fernández' Los Tejanos.[49]

Other examples of Mexican American culture in San Angelo included the presence of "low riders" and "cholos." These groups were composed of a very small minority of barrio boys who borrowed styles from Mexican Americans living in other parts of the country.

The low rider movement began in Los Angeles barrios in the 1960s and spread to Texas and other states when youths returned from visits to California. Lowriders customized cars and adapted them hydraulically for riding low to the ground. They liked "cruising" down San Angelo streets. A Lowrider Club existed in the 1980s and met regularly.[50]

Cholos similarly duplicated styles from the West Coast. Usually a bit younger than lowriders, cholos dressed in a fashion reminiscent of the Zoot Suiters of the 1940s and the pachucos of the 1950s. They wore baggy khaki pants, Stacey-brand shoes, a felt hat with matching hat band, and either a white tanktop t-shirt or a vest with a white button-down dress shirt. Cholos kept their outfit neat and their hair short on the back and sides.[51]

The fiestas patrias celebrations held at the Southside Lions Clubhouse grounds along the South Concho River also testified to the strength of the Mexican American culture. Although no longer as elaborate as they had been under Sedeño's tutelage and now attended by the less assimilated of San Angelo's Hispanic society, the fiestas still lasted for two days with much ado.[52]

Finally, religion remained a strong indicator of Mexican American faithfulness to their cultural past. Although Mexican Protestant churches did well in the city, the greatest percentage of Mexican Americans adhered to Catholicism, the principal religion of Mexico. Of the five Catholic churches in the city, three had almost exclusively Mexican congregations. Sacred Heart, which had been the Mexicans' only church in the 1880s and then segregated in the 1910s, was wholly integrated by the 1980s. While the original St. Mary's building still served the south barrios, St. Joseph in 1983 moved to a new structure which replaced the one built by Father Fidelis' parishioners in 1957.[53]

Other aspects of the Mexicans' religious past were found in such things as the holding of posadas, reenactments of Mary and Joseph's search for an inn at Christmas time;[54] observations of saints' days, and the Fiestas de Nuestra Señora de Guadalupe (Festival of Our Lady of Guadalupe) in December. The latter celebration was usually an all-afternoon Sunday affair held at the San Angelo Coliseum to accommodate the large crowd. It included a mass, a play depicting the apparition of the Virgen de Guadalupe to Juan Diego near Mexico City in December 1531, plus cultural programs featuring folkloric groups, music, and other talent from San Angelo and surrounding areas.[55]

Almost all the Anglo Protestant churches had "Mexican" counterparts in the Hispanic sections of town which ministered in Spanish. The Iglesia Presbiteriana Nazareth (Nazareth Presbyterian Church), for example, sought to adapt Mexican traditions to essentially Anglo services. Under the leadership of the Reverend Tomás Chávez, the church substituted the tortilla for the traditional bread at communion service. Chávez also converted worship into a fiesta-like event.[56]

Finally, in the mid-1980's, members of San Angelo's

Hispanic community could accurately be labeled "Mexican American," for they had assimilated important parts of both cultures.[57] On the one hand, they had borrowed much from Anglos. On the other, they remained proud of their rich ethnic heritage. Equipped with this dual identity, San Angeleños—as they had been doing for more than a century—were able to enrich both themselves and the life of the entire community.[58]

Footnotes

CHAPTER 1

Spanish Activity and Mexican Arrivals

[1]Gus Clemens, *The Concho Country* (San Antonio: Mulberry Avenue Books, 1980), pp. 18-25.

[2]Ibid., p. 53.

[3]Ibid., p. 59.

[4]Ibid., p. 60.

[5]Ibid., p. 84.

[6]Bill Green, *The Dancing Was Lively: Fort Concho, Texas, A Social History, 1867-1882* (San Angelo: Fort Concho Sketches Publishing Co., 1974), p. 30.

[7]Ibid., p. 32.

[8]Clemens, *Concho Country,* p. 60.

[9]Ibid., p. 61.

[10]Ibid., p. 87.

[11]Escal F. Duke, "A Population Study of Tom Green County, 1880," *West Texas Historical Association Yearbook,* LII (1976), 49-60.

[12]Bill Green Papers in possession of author. Essentially, the "Bill Green papers" are correspondence between historian Bill Green, a knowledgeable source of Concho Country history, and Frederick R. Schmidt of Ramona, California. They contain an abundance of information on early Hispanic history in the area, as extracted from Dr. Green's personal notes. Herein they are referred to as the "Bill Green Papers." Copies were provided to the author courtesy of John Estrada family from San Angelo, Texas, and Mrs. Dora Tafolla Estrada from El Cajón, California.

[13]San Angelo *Standard,* June 20, 1924, p. 5; May 3, 1934, p. 4 (Section 4).

[14]Ibid., May 3, 1934, p. 1 (Section 1).

[15]Tom Green County Commissioners' Court Minutes, Volume A, April 7, 1875, Tom Green County Courthouse; San Angelo *Standard,* October 15, 1892, p. 4; May 3, 1924, p. 5 (Section 1); June 20, 1924, p. 5; Bill Green Papers.

[16]Tom Green County Commissioners' Court Minutes, Volume A, April 7, 1875.

[17]Pablo Alderette originally presided over Precinct No. 3 (where his son Guillermo also resided). This was changed to Precinct No. 2 in December 1875. Tom Green County Commissioners' Court Minutes, Volume A, December 23, 1875; San Angelo *Standard,* May 3, 1924, p. 5 (Section 1).

[18]Tom Green County Commissioners' Court Minutes, Volume A, April 7, 1875.

[19]Ibid., April 18, 1876.

[20]Grace Bitner, "The History of Tom Green County, Texas" (Master of Arts Thesis, University of Texas at Austin, 1931), pp. 127-128.

CHAPTER 2

The San Angeleños

[1]Those testifying to this effect include Nathaniel Taylor, in *The Coming Empire, or Two Thousand Miles in Texas on Horseback* (Houston: N. T. Carlisle, 1936), p. 244; and Benjamin H. Grierson, commander of Fort Concho in the 1870s, quoted in Green, *The Dancing was Lively,* p. 62.

Santa Ángela in that period was a general center of vice and prostitution. Some who lived in the town, including Anglos, blacks, and Mexicans, offered sex and drink, among other things, to those calling for it in an isolated frontier setting. See Greg Melton, "Trials by Nature: The Harsh Environment of Fort Concho, Texas" (Master of Arts Thesis, Abilene Christian University, 1981), Chapter 7, entitled, "Booze, Brothels and Brawls."

Footnotes

[2]Green, *The Dancing was Lively,* p. 62; Robert G. Carter, *On the Border with MacKenzie; or, Winning West Texas from the Comanches* (Washington, D.C.: Eynon Printing Co., 1935), p. 54.

[3]Clemens, *The Concho Country,* p. 85; Wayne Daniel, "San Angelo Receives a New Name," *Scene,* Weekly Supplement of San Angelo *Standard-Times,* November 6-7, 1980, p. 3.

[4]Interviews with Gus Clemens, November 24, 1982; Bill Green, November 17, 1982; and Nicolás Flores, October 20, 1982.

[5]Interviews with Nicolás Flores and Gus Clemens.

[6]Clemens, *The Concho Country,* pp. 90-91.

[7]Interviews with Bill Green and Gus Clemens.

[8]The Post Office's reason for changing the town's name demonstrates how a little knowledge can be dangerous. When local Anglos submitted the name "San Ángela" to postal authorities, the federal bureaucrats recognized that the masculine "San" was not correct with the feminine noun "Ángela." Instead of substituting the correct Spanish word—"Santa"—they changed the final "a" in Angela to an "o" in an effort to make the noun masculine and thus satisfy dictates of Spanish grammar. Instead, they created a word which does not exist in Spanish. Clemens, *The Concho Country,* pp. 97-100.

[9]The San Angelo *Standard* in the late 1880s and early 1890s reported cutting affrays, business activity, and social events occurring along Oakes Street or east of it. San Angelo *Standard,* December 27, 1884, p. 3; May 14, 1887, p. 4; and September 22, 1894, p. 3.

[10]Ibid., September 21, 1889, p. 1.

[11]Ibid., June 2, 1888, p. 1; September 21, 1889, p. 1.

[12]Interviews with Nicolás Flores, Bill Green, and Gus Clemens.

[13]Interviews with the John Estrada Family, October 27, 1982, and Nicolás Flores.

[14]San Angelo *Standard,* August 29, 1920, p. 2; Bill Green interview.

[15]Bill Green interview.

[16]Interviews with Nicolás Flores, Estrada family, and Eva Camúñez de Tucker, December 10, 1982, and April 4, 1983.

[17]See Appendix for a genealogical chart of the family.

[18]Ibid.

[19]Estrada interview; Cruz Morán interview, September 23, 1982; Ramona Wuertenburg Muela interview, November 10, 1982.

[20]Tom Green County Commissioners' Court Minutes, Volume A, April 7, 1875.

[21]Bitner, "The History of Tom Green County," pp. 127-128.

[22]San Angelo *Standard,* May 9, 1885, p. 3.

[23]Ibid., September 10, 1887, p. 2.

[24]Ibid., September 22, 1894, p. 3; September 21, 1895, p. 3; September 30, 1899, p. 1.

[25]Arnoldo De León, *Las Fiestas Patrias: Biographic Notes on the Hispanic Presence in San Angelo, Texas* (San Antonio: Caravel Press, 1978).

[26]San Angelo *Standard,* January 18, 1896, p. 2.

[27]Ibid., March 24, 1906, p. 11.

[28]San Angelo *Standard-Times,* May 3, 1934, p. 5 (Section 2); *West Texas Angelus,* Catholic Diocese of San Angelo, February 10, 1984, p. 1.

[29]Clemens, *The Concho Country,* p. 101.

[30]*West Texas Angelus,* February 10, 1984, p. 3. This issue contains an excellent history of early day Catholicism in San Angelo and the Concho Country.

[31]Nicolás Flores, Estrada family, and Eva Camúñez de Tucker interviews.

[32]Green, *The Dancing Was Lively,* p. 76.

[33]San Angelo *Standard,* September 21, 1889, p. 1; October 12, 1889, p. 2. A response to MacGowan on this matter may be found in ibid., September 28, 1889, p. 2.

[34]Eva Camúñez de Tucker interviews.

[35]For a short essay describing the scenario of the traditional formality of asking for a bride's hand in marriage, see Guadalupe C. Quintanilla and James B. Silman, *El Espíritu Siempre Eterno del México Americano* (Washington, D.C.: University Press of America, 1977), pp. 17-25.

[36]See genealogy tables in Appendix.

[37]Tom Green County Censuses, 1880-1900, microfilm copies deposited at the Angelo State University Library, San Angelo, Texas.

[38]Among these was the rather glamorous wedding of Jesús Tafolla and Felipa Romo in 1906. San Angelo *Standard,* February 3, 1906, p. 3.

[39]Nicolás Flores and Cruz Morán interviews.

[40]San Angelo *Standard,* September 21, 1889, p. 1.

[41]El Paso *Times,* El Paso, Texas, July 22, 1886, p. 3.

[42]San Angelo *Standard,* February 6, 1904, p. 7. See also issues of October 20, 1894, p. 1; October 27, 1894, p. 1; May 17, 1902, p. 6; June 6, 1903, p. 7, where other references to Mexicans in politics are made.

[43]San Angelo was first incorporated as a city in 1889. Incorporation was then abolished; the town was reincorporated in 1892, abolished again in 1897, and incorporated again in 1903. San Angelo *Standard-Times,* June 27, 1982, p. 47G.

[44]James Diego Vigil, *From Indians to Chicanos: A Socio-cultural History* (St. Louis: C. V. Mosley, 1980), p. 186.

[45]San Angelo *Standard,* September 30, 1899, p. 1.

[46]Ibid., September 11, 1909, p. 2.

[47]Ibid., December 26, 1910, p. 2.

[48]Ibid., March 24, 1906, p. 11.

[49]Tom Green County Census of 1880; San Angelo *Standard-Times* May 3, 1934, p. 3 (Section 4).

[50]Bill Green Papers. The teacher referred to is apparently Mrs. Fannie Steffens, who taught in the Mexican school in the late 1890s. San Angelo *Standard,* February 29, 1896, p. 3.

[51]San Angelo *Standard,* June 22, 1895, p. 3.

[52]Ibid., February 29, 1896, p. 3. See further information in ibid., August 19, 1899, p. 3; September 23, 1899, p. 3; September 6, 1902, p. 1.

[53]Ibid., September 6, 1902, p. 1; January 23, 1904, p. 7.

[54]Ibid., September 10, 1904, p. 2; Clemens, *The Concho Country,* p. 142.

[55]San Angelo *Standard,* September 2, 1905, p. 3; September 9, 1905, p. 8; October 7, 1905, p. 10; November 4, 1905, p. 4; February 10, 1906, p. 9; March 17, 1906, p. 1; April 7, 1906, p. 4; May 5, 1906, p. 4; September 12, 1909, p. 5; September 16, 1909, p. 5.

[56]Ibid., September 2, 1905, p. 3; Clemens, *The Concho Country,* p. 142.

[57]Arnoldo De León, "Blowout 1910 Style: A Chicano School Boycott in West Texas," *Texana,* XII (1974), 126.

[58]Ibid.

[59]Ibid., p. 132. Catholic sponsored schools dated back to the 1880s. Around 1887, the church established St. Peter's School for Mexican students. Bitner, "The History of Tom Green County," pp. 77, 84. In 1895, the Sisters of Charity of the Incarnate Word taught a school with about fifty Mexican children. San Angelo *Standard,* June 22, 1895, p. 3.

[60]De León, "Blowout 1910 Style," p. 133.

[61]The census of 1900 appears unreliable, and the Bureau of the Census did not report the town's population then, since San Angelo was unincorporated between 1897 and 1903. The census figures of 1910 are much more dependable for this study's purpose.

[62]The city directory of 1909 tends to substantiate these patterns, though the figures are not exact. *Worley's Directory of San Angelo, 1909* (compiled and published by John Worley Directory Company, Dallas, Texas, 1909). Collections of these directories are held by the Chamber of Commerce, San Angelo Convention

Center, the Tom Green County Library, and the Fort Concho Museum Library. The 1908 directory is the first in the series.

CHAPTER 3
A New Barrio Appears

[1]Tom Green County Census, 1910, microfilm copies deposited at the Angelo State University Library, San Angelo, Texas.

[2]San Angelo *Standard,* December 8, 1910, p. 1.

[3]Ibid., March 24, 1912, p. 2; May 30, 1910, p. 1; May 27, 1927, p. 2; September 9, 1909, p. 4; September 17, 1918, p. 2.

[4]Ibid., May 23, 1918, p. 2.

[5]Ibid., September 9, 1909, p. 4; January 18, 1911, p. 7; San Angelo *Morning Standard,* September 28, 1928, p. 3.

[6]San Angelo *Standard,* October 27, 1909, p. 11; October 29, 1909, p. 8.

[7]Ibid., September 22, 1914, p. 2.

[8]Ibid., September 15, 1914, p. 1.

[9]Ibid., October 2, 1914, p. 6; October 7, 1914, p. 4; December 30, 1919, p. 1; February 20, 1920, p. 1; March 22, 1920, p. 1.
Wages through the 1920s ranged anywhere from $1.25 to $2.00 per 100 pounds. See *Standard,* October 5, 1919, p. 1; September 24, 1925, p. 1.

[10]Ibid., December 24, 1919, p. 1; December 30, 1919, p. 1; February 20, 1920, p. 1; March 18, 1921, p. 3.

[11]Advertisement poster (circa 1910s) in Fort Concho Library.

[12]San Angelo *Standard,* January 1, 1917, p. 4; August 6, 1922, p. 6 (Section 1); *West Texas Angelus,* February 10, 1984, p. 3; *West Texas Register,* Catholic Diocese of San Angelo, August 24, 1956.

[13]San Angelo *Standard,* May 22, 1915, p. 1; September 22, 1915, p. 1; December 22, 1915, p. 6; April 7, 1916, p. 2; June 1, 1916, p. 2; December 27, 1916, p. 1; May 27, 1917, p. 21; September 10, 1917, p. 2; December 24, 1917, p. 1; March 25, 1918, p. 1; September 5, 1918, p. 4; September 12, 1918, p. 4; May 30, 1919, p. 3; December 17, 1919, p. 1; December 13, 1921, p. 1; January 15, 1923, p. 2; March 20, 1927, p. 11; and B. A. Hodges, *A History of the Mexican Mission Work Conducted by the Presbyterian Church in the United States of America in the Synod of Texas* (Waxahachie: The Woman's Synodical of Texas, 1931), reprinted in Carlos E. Cortes, *Church Views of the Mexican American* (New York: Arno Press, 1974).

[14]San Angelo *Standard,* July 26, 1925, p. 8; July 26, 1925, p. 11; August 3, 1925, p. 2; August 15, 1926, p. 4; February 27, 1927, p. 8; June 24, 1927, p. 9; July 31, 1927, p. 7; San Angelo *Morning Standard,* July 8, 1928, p. 6; July 10, 1928, p. 9; April 26, 1929, p. 9; July 25, 1929, p. 4; July 28, 1929, p. 10; August 23, 1929, p. 14; January 17, 1933, p. 4.

[15]De León, "Blowout 1910 Style."

[16]San Angelo *Standard,* May 31, 1916, p. 1.

[17]Ibid., May 22, 1915, p. 1.

[18]Ibid., June 2, 1915, p. 3.

[19]Ibid., May 27, 1918, p. 2; August 6, 1922, p. 6 (Section 1).

[20]Ibid., May 29, 1921, p. 3; interview with Helen Robles Martínez, May 22, 1984; Worley, *San Angelo City Directory,* 1925, p. 31; *West Texas Register,* August 24, 1956.

[21]San Angelo *Standard,* June 25, 1922 (Section 1); September 3, 1922, p. 3 (Section 2); September 10, 1922, p. 2 (Section 1); San Angelo *Standard-Times,* August 29, 1954, Section E.

[22]San Angelo *Standard,* June 14, 1923, p. 6; September 12, 1923, p. 2; December 21, 1924, p. 7 (Section 1); September 27, 1925, p. 6 (Section 1); Worley, *San Angelo City Directory,* 1923 to 1927.

[23]San Angelo *Standard,* January 13, 1926, p. 3; February 10, 1926, p. 12; San Angelo *Morning Standard,* February 17, 1928, p. 1 (Section 2); March 16, 1928, p. 1 (Section 2).

[24]San Angelo *Morning Standard,* September 15, 1928, p. 5; December 8, 1928, p. 13; March 7, 1929, p. 1; September 6, 1936, p. 13.

Guadalupe Elementary School closed its doors in 1968. San Angelo *Standard-Times,* July 19, 1970, p. 3B.

[25]San Angelo *Morning Standard,* December 8, 1928, p. 13; March 7, 1929, p. 1.

[26]De León, *Las Fiestas Patrias,* pp. 7-8.

[27]Melton, "Trials by Nature: The Harsh Environment of Fort Concho, Texas," Chapter 7; San Angelo *Standard,* May 3, 1924, p. 6; pp. 6, 11 (Section 2).

[28]San Angelo *Standard,* May 9, 1891, pp. 1, 3.

[29]Ibid., February 3, 1906, p. 9.

[30]Cruz Morán interview; San Angelo *Standard,* August 25, 1912, p. 1; June 6, 1920, p. 1 (Section 2).

[31]San Angelo *Standard,* September 26, 1913, p. 1; December 29, 1914, p. 1.

[32]Ibid., May 26, 1922, p. 1; December 4, 1922, p. 1; April 1, 1923, p. 3.

[33]Ibid., April 13, 1911, p. 1; November 16, 1916, p. 1; November 10, 1919, p. 1; February 11, 1921, p. 1.

[34]Ibid., December 16, 1912, p. 1; November 26, 1913, p. 1; January 28, 1914, p. 1.

[35]Ibid., September 6, 1925, p. 1; September 8, 1925, p. 3.

[36]Ibid., January 14, 1912, p. 4; April 21, 1914, p. 1; April 28, 1914, p. 1; May 4, 1914, p. 1; June 2, 1914, p. 1; September 14, 1914, p. 1; September 21, 1914, p. 1.

[37]Sixteenth Census of the United States, *Population,* Vol. I (Washington: Government Printing Office, 1942), p. 1040, Table 2.

[38]San Angelo *Standard,* June 6, 1920, p. 1 (Section 2).

[39]Clemens, *The Concho Country,* p. 138. The downtown area was renovated in the 1980s. San Angelo *Standard-Times,* January 29, 1984, pp. 6G-7G.

[40]Clemens, *The Concho Country,* p. 103.

[41]*San Angelo City Directory,* 1929 through 1939.

CHAPTER 4

Depression and War

[1]Clemens, *The Concho Country,* p. 139.

[2]San Angelo *Morning Standard,* March 1, 1930, p. 9.

[3]Ibid., December 8, 1933, p. 13.

[4]San Angelo *Morning Standard,* June 16, 1931, p. 1A.

During the 1934 Sheepshearers' boycott on area ranches, sheepman threatened to provide relief boards with the names of *tasinques* participating in the work stoppage. See Arnoldo De León, *"Los Tasinques* and the Sheepshearers' Union of North America: A Strike in West Texas, 1934," *West Texas Historical Association Yearbook,* LV (1979), pp. 1-16.

[5]Reynolds McKay, "Texas Mexican Repatriation During the Great Depression" (Ph.D. dissertation, University of Oklahoma 1982), pp. 300; 126-127.

[6]Ibid., p. 103; San Angelo *Morning Standard,* April 16, 1939, p. 1A.

[7]San Angelo *Morning Standard,* April 16, 1939, p. 1A; April 22, 1932, p. 12.

[8]Ibid., April 19, 1935, p. 5.

[9]San Angelo *Standard-Times,* August 29, 1941, p. 1 (Section 2).

[10]Nicolás Flores interview; San Angelo *Morning Standard,* January 18, 1934, p. 2.

[11]San Angelo *Morning Standard,* September 18, 1936, p. 1; September 20, 1936, p. 3.

[12]Ibid., September 16, 1936, p. 3; September 18, 1936, p. 1; September 19, 1936, p. 2.

[13]Fifteenth Census of the United States: 1930, *Population,* Vol. II (Washington

D.C.: Government Printing Office, 1933), p. 90, Table 27. In 1930, Mexicans were not classified as white, but as members of "other races." The number of those listed for San Angelo as "other races" was 2,706.

[14]Sixteenth Census of the United States, *Population,* Vol. I (Washington: Government Printing Office, 1942), p. 1040, Table 2. The population increased from 25,308 inhabitants in 1930 to 25,802 in 1940.

[15]San Angelo *Standard,* May 27, 1918, p. 2; August 28, 1923, p. 2.

[16]San Angelo *Standard-Times,* August 13, 1939, p. 17 (Section 1).

[17]San Angelo *Morning Standard,* January 9, 1930, p. 1; January 15, 1930, p. 1; April 12, 1930, p. 1 (Section 2); September 7, 1930, p. 3 (Section 1); May 9, 1934, p. 1.

[18]Ibid., September 9, 1928 (Section 1).

[19]Ibid., May 12, 1929, p. 24 (Section 1).

[20]Ibid., June 22, 1930, p. 2; August 9, 1931, p. 14.

[21]Ibid., August 9, 1931, p. 14; August 12, 1931. p. 7.

[22]Ibid., December 13, 1936, p. 9 (Section 1).

[23]Correspondence with Ed Idar Jr., June 19, 1984.

[24]San Angelo *Standard-Times,* November 24, 1940, p. 9. A Ladies Council (No. 31) of LULAC was organized in May 1940. See Ibid., May 19, 1940, p. 3; June 16, 1940, p. 2.

[25]Ibid., September 28, 1930, p. 7.

[26]Ibid., June 16, 1940, p. 2 (Section 1); August 26, 1940, p. 7; June 30, 1940, p. 2 (Section 1); November 14, 1941, p. 14.

[27]Interview with Henry V. Vélez, May 22, 1984; interview with Máximo Guerrero, June 22, 1984. The San Angelo *Standard* carried the announcement of the program in both the morning and evening editions from approximately December 26, 1936, to January 14, 1937. See particularly the *Morning Standard,* January 10, 1937, and San Angelo *Evening Standard,* December 29, 1936, p. 4.

[28]See enrollment figures in the following editions of the San Angelo *Morning Times:* September 13, 1929, p. 18 (Section 1); February 11, 1932, p. 9; November 8, 1934, p. 10; March 6, 1935, p. 4; May 3, 1935, p. 3; September 22, 1935, p. 6 (Section 1); May 5, 1937, p. 9; April 7, 1938, p. 7; February 10, 1939, p. 24; San Angelo *Standard-Times,* September 7, 1941, p. 6 (Section 1); September 10, 1941, p. 7 (Section 1); and September 9, 1942, p. 13.

[29]San Angelo *Standard-Times,* August 29, 1954, Section E.

[30]San Angelo *Morning Standard,* September 9, 1934, p. 2 (Section 2); June 16, 1935, p. 2 (Section 2); September 6, 1936, p. 13 (Section 2); September 2, 1938, p. 18; San Angelo *Standard-Times,* January 26, 1941, p. 2; May 25, 1941, p. 2; November 14, 1941, p. 14.

[31]San Angelo *Morning Standard,* May 25, 1938, p. 5; May 25, 1939, p. 7; May 23, 1940, p. 14.

[32]Interview with Eva Camúñez de Tucker; San Angelo *Morning Standard,* April 21, 1929, p. 1 (Section 2); *Los Tiempos,* San Angelo, Texas, December 14, 1983, p. 1. Also graduating in 1930 was Gloria Effie Ruiz, daughter of the Baptist minister, Reverend Donato Ruiz, who apparently had received her early education elsewhere. The Ruizes had come to the city from San Marcos in the mid-1920s. *Morning Standard,* May 22, 1930, p. 10; San Angelo *Standard-Times,* December 12, 1943, p. 3.

[33]San Angelo *Morning Standard,* May 18, 1935, p. 11; interview with Helen Robles Martinez, May 22, 1984.

[34]San Angelo *Standard-Times,* May 24, 1940, p. 20; March 20, 1938, p. 10; April 24, 1938, p. 12.

[35]Ibid., March 29, 1942, p. 10 (Section 2).

[36]Ibid., May 23, 1943, p. 2 (Section 1).

[37]Arnoldo De León, "St. Joseph's Church: A History," in *St. Joseph Church* (San Angelo: Memorial Dedication Book, 1983).

[38]Estrada family interview; Nicolás Flores interview; Cruz Morán interview, Eva Camúñez de Tucker interview.

[39]San Angelo *Standard-Times,* December 12, 1943, p. 3.

[40]Ibid., January 26, 1941, p. 6; February 2, 1941, p. 4 (Section 1); January 19, 1945, p. 21; January 21, 1945, p. 4 (Section 1).

[41]Ibid., June 4, 1944, p. 7 (Section 1).

[42]San Angelo *Morning Standard,* June 26, 1936, p. 18; Tomás Chávez Jr., *Texas Mexican Presbyterians* (Midland, Texas: First Presbyterian Church Press, 1980), p. 29.

[43]San Angelo *Morning Standard,* April 16, 1938, p. 7.

[44]San Angelo *Standard-Times,* December 24, 1944, p. 2 (Section 2).

[45]Ibid., May 14, 1944, p. 8 (Section 1).

[46]De León, *Las Fiestas Patrias,* pp. 8-11.

[47]San Angelo *Morning Times,* May 17, 1932, p. 7; June 14, 1932, p. 13.

[48]Ibid., July 21, 1933, p. 8; March 30, 1934, p. 6; August 6, 1936, p. 6; October 1, 1936, p. 7; May 27, 1937, p. 6.

[49]Ibid., February 25, 1938, p. 10; San Angelo *Standard-Times,* November 5, 1941, p. 8.

[50]San Angelo *Morning Standard,* March 20, 1938, p. 10 (Section 1); April 24, 1938, p. 12 (Section 1).

[51]San Angelo *Standard-Times,* August 26, 1940, p. 7.

[52]Ibid., July 10, 1942, p. 1 (Section 2); September 27, 1942, p. 1 (Section 1); August 31, 1947, p. 10; July 27, 1945, p. 2; *Los Tiempos,* January 11, 1984, p. 1.

[53]Correspondence with Mario J. Cruz, February 27, 1984.

[54]San Angelo *Standard-Times,* July 25, 1944, p. 1; November 26, 1944, p. 1.

[55]Ibid., May 11, 1948, p. 18; August 26, 1949, p. 1.

[56]Mario J. Cruz correspondence, February 27, 1984.

[57]San Angelo *Standard-Times,* December 14, 1941, p. 4 (Section 1); June 7, 1942, p. 5 (Section 1); February 12, 1943, p. 6; August 18, 1943, p. 5; September 23, 1945, p. 1; November 23, 1946, p. 25.

CHAPTER 5
The G.I. Generation in Years of Flux

[1]San Angelo *Standard-Times,* November 27, 1945, p. 2.

[2]Ibid., August 14, 1945, p. 3.

[3]Ibid., August 5, 1945, p. 6; August 14, 1945, p. 3; September 11, 1945, p. 1.

[4]Ibid., November 27, 1945, p. 2; September 11, 1945, p. 1; correspondence with Mrs. Aurora Garcia, May 2, 1984.

[5]San Angelo *Standard-Times,* January 10, 1946, p. 11.

[6]Ibid., January 12, 1946, p. 1.

[7]Ibid., August 25, 1949, p. 1; September 30, 1949, p. 1; Minutes of the City Commission, vol. 18, pp. 161-166, City Secretary's Office, City Hall, San Angelo, Texas.

[8]San Angelo *Standard-Times,* July 27, 1945, p. 2.

[9]Alonso Perales, *Are We Good Neighbors?* (San Antonio: Artes Gráficas, 1948), pp. 168-169, 220.

[10]San Angelo *Evening Standard,* September 10, 1945, p. 1; September 11, 1945, p. 1.

[11]San Angelo *Standard-Times,* September 8, 1945, p. 12; September 11, 1945, p. 1. Perales, *Are We Good Neighbors?,* pp. 173-174.

[12]Anonymous interview in author's file.

[13]San Angelo *Standard-Times,* September 11, 1945, p. 2.

[14]San Angelo *Evening Standard,* September 10, 1945, p. 4A; Correspondence with Mrs. Aurora Garcia, May 2, 1984.

[15]San Angelo *Standard-Times,* September 15, 1945, p. 3.

[16]This section on LULAC No. 152 relies heavily on documents provided by Frank

Footnotes

A. Martinez. Copies are in author's possession. Also, interview with Henry V. Vélez, May 22, 1984.

For a description of the lamentable conditions at Sam Houston Elementary School in 1946, see San Angelo *Standard-Times,* January 12, 1946, p. 12.

[17]Carl Allsup, *The American G.I. Forum,* Center for Mexican American Studies, Monograph 6 (Austin: University of Texas Press, 1982), pp. 33-38.

[18]Correspondence with Mario J. Cruz, February 27, 1984.

[19]San Angelo *Standard-Times,* September 3, 1948, p. 17.

[20]Interview with Pete Chapa, May 23, 1984. San Angelo *Standard-Times,* February 14, 1954, p. 1; February 15, 1954, p. 1; June 21, 1959, p. 9C; San Angelo *Evening Standard,* June 19, 1957, p. 9; June 26, 1957, p. 8.

[21]San Angelo *Standard-Times,* April 1, 1950, p. 1; April 12, 1950, p. 12.

[22]Ibid., April 1, 1950, p. 1.

[23]Ibid., March 15, 1951, p. 7.

[24]Ibid., March 18, 1951, p. 10.

[25]Ibid., March 15, 1951, p. 7.

[26]Ibid., March 16, 1951, p. 14.

[27]Ibid., April 1, 1951, p. 6A.

[28]Correspondence with Mario J. Cruz, February 27, 1984.

[29]San Angelo *Standard-Times,* March 18, 1951, p. 10.

[30]Ibid., March 25, 1951, p. 4H.

[31]Worley, *San Angelo City Directories,* 1952 through 1954. Rosaura G. Gonzales taught music throughout the school district in 1955-1956.

[32]San Angelo *Standard-Times,* November 10, 1957, p. 8C; September 7, 1958, p. 6D; October 11, 1959, p. 6C; August 18, 1962, p. 2A.

[33]Correspondence with Mario J. Cruz, February 27, 1984.

[34]San Angelo *Standard-Times,* May 27, 1951, p. 10.

[35]Ibid., May 21, 1956, p. 10.

[36]Ibid., June 2, 1946, p. 4.

[37]Ibid., May 24, 1958, p. 5.

[38]Ibid., June 10, 1959, p. 1B.

[39]Ibid., November 15, 1958, p. 3B.

[40]Ibid., August 11, 1946, p. 9.

[41]Ibid., March 25, 1951, p. 4H.

[42]Ibid., March 29, 1949, p. 20B; June 1, 1947, p. 22; Chávez, *Texas Mexican Presbyterians,* p. 29.

[43]San Angelo *Standard-Times,* June 22, 1946, p. 12; July 31, 1947, p. 2.

[44]Ibid., August 14, 1945, p. 3.

[45]Ibid., September 11, 1945, p. 2.

[46]De León, "St. Joseph's Church: A History."

[47]De León, *Las Fiestas Patrias,* pp. 15-19.

[48]San Angelo *Standard-Times,* August 26, 1949, p. 1; March 17, 1952, p. 7.

[49]Ibid., December 8, 1950, p. 12.

[50]Ibid., October 15, 1952, p. 2.

CHAPTER 6

New Horizons

[1]Eighteenth Census of the United States, *Census of Population: 1960,* Volume I, Part A (Washington, D.C.: Government Printing Office, 1961), p. 45-23, Table 5.

[2]*San Angelo Comprehensive Plan, Part I* (San Angelo: Department of Planning, 1977), p. 21. This document estimated that Mexican Americans amounted to 14 percent of the city's total 1960 population.

[3]San Angelo *Standard-Times,* May 31, 1958, p. 1B.

[4]Ibid., May 26, 1960, p. 1A; June 26, 1960, p. 1.

[5]Correspondence with Ed Idar Jr., March 28, 1984; San Antonio *Express,* July 16, 1972, p. 6B.

[6]San Angelo *Evening Times,* August 28, 1980, p. 1A; Ed Idar Jr. correspondence, March 28, 1984.

[7]San Angelo *Standard-Times,* March 31, 1962, p. 1B; April 8, 1962, p. 1A; May 6, 1962, p. 1.

[8]Ibid., March 31, 1962, p. 1B; January 10, 1965, p. 13A.

[9]Correspondence with Ed Idar Jr., March 28, 1984; Pete Chapa interview, May 23, 1984.

[10]San Angelo *Standard-Times,* February 26, 1964, p. 2A.

[11]Ibid., April 5, 1964, p. 1A.

[12]For a brief historical overview of the Idar family, see San Antonio *Express,* July 16, 1972, p. 6B. This piece also contains a lengthy biographical sketch of Ed Idar Jr.

[13]San Angelo *Standard-Times,* April 2, 1966, p. 2A.

[14]Ibid., May 8, 1966, p. 2A. Also running in the 1966 county election (Precinct 4) was Eli Martinez. Ibid.

[15]Correspondence with Ed Idar Jr., March 28, 1984; San Antonio *Express,* July 16, 1972, p. 6B; and story in San Angelo *Standard-Times,* date unknown, in author's file. Idar left San Angelo in 1968 to take a position with the Office of Economic Opportunity in Austin. San Antonio *Express,* July 16, 1972, p. 6B.

[16]San Angelo *Standard-Times,* September 5, 1962, p. 7A; correspondence with Ed Idar Jr., March 28, 1984; San Antonio *Express,* July 16, 1972, p. 6B.

[17]San Angelo *Standard-Times,* May 5, 1962, p. 8A; April 29, 1962, p. 7A.

[18]Ibid., January 16, 1963, p. 5A.

[19]Ibid., January 24, 1962, p. 2B. See also, ibid., May 23, 1960, p. 4A.

[20]Ibid., January 30, 1962, p. 6A; August 26, 1962, p. 4A.

[21]Ibid., December 7, 1961, p. 1A; January 28, 1962, p. 1; April 29, 1962, p. 7A; May 14, 1962, p. 5A; August 26, 1962, p. 4A; October 31, 1962, p. 11A; November 25, 1962, p. 11A; January 18, 1963, p. 10A; February 24, 1963, p. 10D; April 15, 1963, p. 1A.

[22]Interview with Oscar C. Gómez, February 25, 1984.

[23]San Angelo *Standard-Times,* June 21, 1963, p. 1B; July 4, 1963, p. 1B; July 5, 1963, p. 14A; July 6, 1963, pp. 2A, 1B; July 7, 1963, p. 1B; July 7, 1963, p. 7C.

[24]Interview with Raymond Holguín, January 9, 1984; *Los Tiempos,* January 18, 1984, p. 1; Correspondence with Ed Idar Jr., March 28, 1984.

[25]De León, *Las Fiestas Patrias,* p. 21.

[26]Interview with Raymond Holguín.

[27]*Los Tiempos,* May 16, 1984, p. 1. A meeting between Armando Figueroa and Henry V. Vélez with the school board following the incident produced an agreement from school officials that thenceforth the German dance was not to be publicized as a school activity. Henry V. Vélez interview, May 22, 1984.

[28]San Angelo *Standard-Times,* May 25, 1975, p. 3A; May 17, 1977, p. 7B.

[29]Ibid., August 13, 1968, p. 4A.

[30]Ibid., March 9, 1969, p. 12D.

[31]Ibid., April 11, 1966, p. 3B; June 17, 1966, p. 1B; March 16, 1968, p. 2A; July 2, 1968, p. 1A; correspondence with Mario J. Cruz, February 27, 1984; San Angelo *Standard-Times,* March 3, 1971, p. 1; March 9, 1971, p. 2A.

[32]San Angelo *Evening Times,* October 28, 1969, p. 4A.

[33]San Angelo *Standard-Times,* June 11, 1967, p. 1C; June 13, 1967, p. 5A; June 14, 1967, p. 6C; June 15, 1967, p. 1B; June 18, 1967, p. 3B.

[34]Ibid., October 31, 1967, p. 1B.

[35]For example, in February 1967, Armando Figueroa, in behalf of himself and "several of the Latin American leaders in San Angelo," forwarded letters to State Senator Dorsey Hardeman and State Representative Forrest A. Harding, asking that they both press for hiring more Mexican Americans in the Department of Public Safety (DPS). The issue involved proposed legislation (by Bob Armstrong of Austin) allowing the DPS to hire out-of-state personnel without the one-year residence requirement. Figueroa and his supporters argued that the DPS should in-

stead dip into the pool of qualified Mexican Americans in the state. Letters in the possession of the author, compliments of Armando Figueroa, May 6, 1984.

Two years later, on July 20, 1969, Figueroa, Arnold Garcia Sr., and two others approached a DPS official in San Angelo about the matter of increased arrests among Mexican Americans for DWI. The group wanted to know if the DPS was "picking on Mexicans" disproportionately. San Angelo *Standard-Times,* July 20, 1969, p. 4A.

Furthermore, these men of the G.I. generation continued employing the technique of getting delegations to go before institutions to discuss issues pertinent to the Mexican American community. Henry V. Vélez interview, May 22, 1984.

CHAPTER 7
Chicano Years

[1]José Limón, "The Folk Performance of 'Chicano' and the Cultural Limits of Political Ideology," in Richard Bauman and Roger D. Abrahams, *"And Other Neighborly Names": Social Process and Cultural Image in Texas Folklore* (Austin: University of Texas Press, 1981), 197-225. For the feelings of three young Angelo State University students on the meaning of the "Chicano Movement," see San Angelo *Evening Times,* October 28, 1971, p. 1A.

[2]San Angelo *Standard-Times,* August 17, 1969, p. 3D; *San Angelo Comprehensive Plan, Part 1,* pp. 21, 22-23, 29.

[3]*San Angelo Comprehensive Plan, Part I,* pp. 21, 23, 26-27, 84, and appendixes B. 2, B. 5, and B. 7.

[4]San Angelo *Standard-Times,* August 30, 1967, p. 8A.

[5]Ibid., October 30, 1969, p. 6A.

[6]The Chicano Student Organization was not without precedent at ASU in the late 1960s. In 1968, students Mario J. Cruz (later a public school counselor in Austin, Texas), Mike Torres (later a Ph.D in genetics), Arnold Garcia, Jr. (later a reporter for the Austin *Statesman*), and Manuel Luján (the registrar at ASU in the 1980s) founded a college fraternity named Alpha Epsilon. Organized because Mexican Americans were not invited into the other fraternities on campus, Alpha Epsilon sought to help Mexican Americans overcome homesickness and to assist them in making the transition to college life. But it also pressed the question of affirmative action at ASU and other issues that would lead to social betterment of Mexican Americans in general. Correspondence with Mario J. Cruz, February 27, 1984.

[7]San Angelo *Standard-Times,* January 4, 1970, p. 5B; January 11, 1970, p. 4B.

[8]Ibid., March 5, 1970, p. 4B.

[9]Ibid., April 5, 1970, p. 1A; May 10, 1970, p. 1A.

[10]Ibid., June 7, 1970, p. 4A.

[11]Ibid., July 18, 1970, p. 2A.

[12]For the numerous letters sent to the *Standard-Times* on the topic of the Precinct 14 episode, see ibid., June 12, 1970, p. 4B; July 22, 1970, p. 4A; July 25, 1970, p. 8A; July 27, 1970, p. 4A; July 30, 1970, p. 10A; August 2, 1970, p. 2C; August 5, 1970, p. 8A; August 6, 1970, p. 8A; August 7, 1970, p. 2B; August 14, 1970, p. 4A.

[13]Ibid., August 4, 1970, p. 7B.

[14]Ibid., August 8, 1970, p. 4B; February 28, 1974, p. 2A. San Angelo *Evening Times,* August 7, 1970, p. 12B. See also the editorial in ibid., p. 2B.

[15]San Angelo *Standard-Times,* October 21, 1970, p. 2A.

[16]Ibid., February 20, 1971, p. 2A.

[17]Ibid., March 3, 1971, p. 5B; interview with Richard V. Garcia, December 29, 1983.

[18]San Angelo *Standard-Times,* September 26, 1971, p. 12B.

[19]Ibid., November 24, 1971, p. 12B.

[20]Ibid., November 1, 1971, p. 2A.

[21]Ibid., October 27, 1971, p. 12A.

[22]Ibid., February 15, 1972, p. 1B.
[23]Ibid., March 20, 1972, p. 1A; March 29, 1972, p. 1A.
[24]Ibid., January 7, 1972, p. 6A; April 1, 1972, p. 5A.
[25]Ibid., April 5, 1972, p. 6C.
[26]Ibid., March 30, 1972, p. 1A; May 6, 1972, p. 1B.
[27]Ibid., August 11, 1972, p. 1B; August 28, 1972, p. 1A.
[28]Ibid., September 4, 1972, p. 6A.
[29]Ibid., September 10, 1972, p. 7A.
[30]Ibid., February 22, 1973, p. 1A; April 5, 1973, p. 4D. See note 26, Chapter 8, for an elaboration on the case of *Regester* v. *White.*
[31]Ibid., March 8, 1973, p. 2A.
[32]Ibid., April 6, 1973, p. 11B.
[33]Ibid., May 6, 1973, p. 1A; *Los Tiempos,* December 28, 1983, p. 1.
[34]San Angelo *Standard-Times,* January 15, 1974, p. 1B.
[35]Ibid., February 5, 1974, p. 11A.
[36]Ibid., April 7, 1974, p. 1A; May 10, 1974, p. 1A; May 12, 1974, p. 1A; May 30, 1974, p. 13A; June 2, 1974, p. 1A.
[37]Ibid., November 30, 1973, p. 10A.
[38]Ibid., June 1, 1975, p. 5A; June 20, 1976, p. 3B.
[39]Pete Chapa interview; Henry V. Vélez interview.
[40]San Angelo *Standard-Times,*October 12, 1975, p. 1D; October 19, 1975, p. 1A, 1B.
[41]Ibid., January 25, 1976, p. 5D; April 24, 1976, p. 3B; June 3, 1977, p. 3B; June 4, 1977, p. 2B.

CHAPTER 8

Towards Equality

[1]San Angelo *Standard-Times,* October 19, 1972, p. 16B.
[2]Ibid., May 4, 1973, p. 6A; February 18, 1973, p. 13A.
[3]Ibid., November 21, 1982, p. 3B.
[4]Ibid., September 1, 1973, p. 2A; June 15, 1974, p. 2A; April 20, 1980, p. 3C.
[5]Ibid., April 28, 1982, p. 8C.
[6]Ibid., February 5, 1983, p. 5B; February 7, 1983, p. 6B; February 14, 1983, p. 4B; February 16, 1983, p. 1A; March 2, 1983, p. 1A; March 8, 1983, p. 1A; August 21, 1983, p. 1A.
[7]Ibid., June 4, 1974, p. 2A; February 2, 1975, p. 1D; March 2, 1975, p. 8A; March 11, 1975, p. 1A.
[8]Ibid., December 5, 1976, p. 11C; January 7, 1977, p. 3A; July 10, 1977, p. 5A.
[9]Ibid., July 9, 1977, p. 3A.
[10]Ibid., February 11, 1981, p. 1B; February 12, 1981, p. 8A (editorial).
[11]Ibid., January 26, 1983, p. 1C; San Angelo *Evening Times,* January 27, 1983, p. 6A (editorial).
[12]San Angelo *Standard-Times,* May 2, 1978, p. 3A; May 6, 1978, p. 3A.
[13]In the 1980s, the Evelio F. Villarreal G.I. Forum, as the local chapter was now called, consisted of only a small group of men, most of them of G.I. generation vintage. Some doubled as members of LULAC. Periodically, Forumeers voiced positions on issues such as bilingual education. Ibid., April 13, 1981, p. 8B; April 19, 1981, p. 1A; San Angelo *Evening Times,* June 29, 1981, p. 2A; June 30, 1981, p. 2A.
[14]San Angelo *Standard-Times,* October 22, 1981, p. 1C; November 3, 1981, p. 4B; November 5, 1981, p. 2C; November 6, 1981, p. 1A; November 10, 1981, p. 5B; November 17, 1981, p. 1A; November 21, 1981, p. 2B; December 5, 1981, p. 1A; January 20, 1982, p. 1B; January 26, 1982, p. 1A; January 27, 1982, p. 1A; March 16, 1982, p. 8B.
[15]Ibid., March 5, 1978, p. 1A; March 8, 1978, p. 1A; March 9, 1978, p. 4A; March 16, 1978, p. 1A; copies of LULAC papers in possession of the author.

Footnotes

[16]San Angelo *Standard-Times,* February 22, 1975, p. 4B; April 6, 1975, p. 1A; *Los Tiempos,* January 25, 1984, p. 1.

[17]San Angelo *Standard-Times,* April 6, 1975, p.1A.

[18]Ibid., March 3, 1977, p. 1A; April 3, 1977, p. 1A.

[19]Ibid., March 30, 1980 (Section C); May 4, 1980, p. 1A.

[20]Ibid., March 29, 1981, p. 3C; April 5, 1981, p. 1A.

[21]Ibid., January 20, 1982, p. 1A; May 2, 1982, p. 4A.

[22]Ibid., January 17, 1982, p. 1A; May 2, 1982, p. 4A.

[23]Ibid., March 28, 1983, p. 5B.

[24]April 6, 1975, p. 1A; April 3, 1977, p. 1A; February 23, 1977, p. 3A; April 1, 1978, p. 1A; *Los Tiempos,* December 28, 1983, p. 1.

[25]Correspondence with Cato Cedillo, May 23, 1984.

[26]San Angelo *Standard-Times,* April 4, 1976, p. 1A; *San Angelo Magazine,* San Angelo, Texas, February 1983.

Ed Idar Jr., who had been in San Angelo in the 1960s, represented MALDEF (Mexican American Legal Defense and Educational Fund) in February 1973 before the United States Supreme Court in arguing the single-member district case apropos to Béxar County House members (*Regester* v. *White*). The MALDEF victory led other counties such as Lubbock, El Paso, Nueces, and Travis to pursue litigation which brought single-member districts there.

When Congress in 1975 extended the Voting Rights Act and made Texas subject to it, the Act empowered the United States Department of Justice to preclear situations where there was the likelihood of diluting the voting strength of minority groups. During committee hearings in Congress, the arguments and evidence which MALDEF used in *Regester* v. *White* were referred to and became part of the "legislative history" of the act. This had substantial impact in convincing Congress to bring Texas under the Act.

Thereafter, many cities and other political subdivisions such as school boards adopted single-member districts either voluntarily or as a result of being coerced to do so under the Voting Rights Act. There was the fear that minorities would complain to the Department of Justice and bring the federal government's wrath upon the local community. It was the above current of events which led Mrs. Cardenas to take the initiative to bring single-member districts to San Angelo in 1976. Correspondence with Ed Idar Jr., June 19, 1984; San Antonio *Express,* December 30, 1973; and *White* v. *Regester,* 93 Supreme Court Reporter 2332.

[27]San Angelo *Standard-Times,* April 2, 1978, p. 6B; January 20, 1978, p. 1A.

[28]San Angelo *Evening Times,* August 28, 1980, p. 1A.

[29]San Angelo *Standard-Times,* March 28, 1982, p. 1C; April 4, 1982, p. 1A.

[30]Ibid., May 19, 1983, p. 2B; December 26, 1982, p. 4C.

[31]San Angelo *Standard-Times,* May 31, 1984, p. 1A; June 2, 1984, p. 1A; June 3, 1984, p. 1A; San Angelo *Evening Times,* May 31, 1984, p. 1A; *Los Tiempos,* April 25, 1984, p. 1.

[32]San Angelo *Standard-Times,* September 25, 1982, p. 1B.

[33]*Los Tiempos,* February 1, 1984, p. 1; May 9, 1984, p. 1.

[34]Program of Commencement Exercises, Central High School, May 24, 1984.

[35]San Angelo *Standard-Times,* May 14, 1983, p. 5B.

[36]Ibid., December 5, 1976, p. 11C; January 7, 1977, p. 3A; January 8, 1977, p. 3A; July 9, 1977, p. 3A; July 10, 1977, p. 5A.

[37]Ibid., October 27, 1978, p. 12A; *Los Tiempos,* February 22, 1984, p. 1; February 29, 1984, p. 1.

[38]*Los Tiempos,* December 21, 1983, p. 3.

[39]For a comprehensive description of life in the San Angelo barrio in the 1980s, see San Angelo *Standard-Times,* December 26, 1982, Section C.

[40]Ibid., December 26, 1982, Section C.

[41]*Los Tiempos,* September 14, 1983, p. 1.

[42]San Angelo *Standard-Times,* November 18, 1973, p. 12E; January 4, 1978, p. 8B.

[43]Chávez, *Mexican American Presbyterians*, p. 30; San Angelo *Standard-Times*, August 25, 1974, p. 3A; May 12, 1979, p. 10A; July 25, 1981, p. 11A; March 13, 1983, p. 4C; December 26, 1982, p. 4C; *Los Tiempos*, November 30, 1983, p. 6; December 28, 1983, p. 1; January 11, 1984, p. 1.

[44]San Angelo *Standard-Times*, March 8, 1983, p. 1A.

[45]Name of informant withheld by request.

[46]WFAA TV, Channel 8, Dallas, Texas, May 7, and May 8, 1984 telecasts.

[47]Taken from the San Angelo *Standard-Times*, December 26, 1982, citing the 1980 census. Hispanics comprised 23 percent of San Angelo's 73,240 population. San Angelo *Standard-Times*, March 31, 1984, p. 1, also citing 1980 census figures.

[48]Ibid., January 18, 1983, p. 1A; January 25, 1983, p. 6A. Furthermore, a movement was initiated by a group of Hispanic businessmen in the city to establish a new Spanish-language radio station. Ibid., March 3, 1983, p. 1A.

[49]San Angelo *Standard-Times*, December 26, 1982, p. 3C; *Los Tiempos*, December 28, 1983, p. 1.

[50]San Angelo *Standard-Times*, June 27, 1981, p. 4B; February 21, 1983, p. 6B; *Los Tiempos*, November 16, 1983, p. 1.

[51]San Angelo *Standard-Times*, February 21, 1983, p. 6B; December 26, 1982, p. 3C.

[52]Ibid., September 15, 1981, p. 3B; September 14, 1982, p. 2A; September 15, 1983, p. 1A; May 4, 1983, Section F.

[53]Ibid., August 15, 1983, p. 1A.

[54]*Los Tiempos*, November 30, 1983, p. 1.

[55]San Angelo *Standard-Times*, December 11, 1977, p. 4A; December 8, 1978, p. 7C; December 11, 1978, p. 3A; December 13, 1982, p. 4B; *Los Tiempos*, November 30, 1983, p. 6; December 14, 1983, p. 1.

[56]Chávez, *Mexican American Presbyterians*, p. 30; San Angelo *Standard-Times*, July 25, 1981, p. 11A.

[57]For an elaboration of the concept of "biculturation," see Arnoldo De León, *The Tejano Community, 1836-1900* (Albuquerque: University of New Mexico Press, 1982), p. xii.

Appendix

Individual Families

Pablo Alderette

Pablo Alderette arrived in the Concho Country in 1869 or 1870, bringing with him parts of four families. These included his wife Ramona and their children, Severa and Jesusita; his son Guillermo, a product of his first marriage in New Mexico; José Ángel Alderette, an adopted son; and four stepchildren, Catalina, Nestor, Charles, and Phillipi, the offspring of Ramona by her first husband, Philip J. Wuertemburg. The entire extended family settled on farm acreage along the North Concho River, where five more children were born to Pablo and Ramona Alderette.

It was from this ranch that Pablo Alderette made a mark on Concho Country politics. In 1875, he was selected one of the first four Tom Green County commissioners and served as a precinct judge during the same period.

By his own initiative and resolve, Pablo made a go of his presence in the Concho Country. Arriving at a time when the region was just developing, he settled his family on unclaimed land, then successfully developed his claim. By 1880, Alderette owned 400 acres of land valued at $6,000 and possessed numerous other assets, including livestock and farming machinery. Upon his death in 1882, the land passed on to Guillermo, his oldest son.[1]

Guillermo proved to be a success story in his own right. While working the Alderette farm with his father and the rest of the family, he engaged in buffalo hunting north of Santa Ángela and operated mule wagons between the young town and San Antonio. With an eye for turning a profit, he bought lots in the heart of Santa Ángela from Bart DeWitt in 1874 (the corner where the old San Angelo National Bank is located) and sold it for a huge profit ten years later. In the latter 1870s, he purchased additional farm land close to his father's spread.[2]

Politics also interested Guillermo. In 1875, he served on the first grand jury in Tom Green County, and his home served as a polling place for elections in 1876.

Guillermo and his family moved to the city in the latter half of the 1880s, apparently settling on land acquired on Twohig Avenue between Irving and Randolph Streets. During this time he operated a saddle horse pasture on his downtown holdings;[3] his property was valued at $5,530 in October 1886.[4] By 1888, he was operating the Red Jacket Saloon.[5] The tax rolls of 1890 show him still the owner of the ranch lands on the North Concho and indicate his taxable property was worth almost $4,000. When killed in 1891 at the Corner Saloon by a watchman at the establishment,[6] he apparently left his lands on the North Concho intact to his wife Ricarda, for the tax rolls continue to indicate her as owning the property.[7] In the fall of 1897 and the spring of 1898, the widow sold the ranch to M. B. Pulliam for some $4,000.[8] The remaining

Alderette property then included the "home lot" on Twohig[9] and another smaller lot in the Santa Fe barrio.[10] In 1927, Ricarda sold the Twohig property—the downtown area was undergoing "modernization"—and moved to 13th Street.[11]

All of Guillermo and Ricarda's boys died violently. William Alderette Jr., was thrown from a horse in 1898, and a deputy constable shot Antonio Alderette in January, 1906.[12] The remaining two, Pablo and Ajeo, were cut down by gunfire in 1912 and 1913.[13]

[1]Bill Green Papers.

[2]Ibid.; San Angelo *Standard,* October 4, 1884, p. 5; Tom Green County Tax Rolls, 1878, 1880, 1885, 1890.

[3]San Angelo *Morning Times,* September 9, 1928, p. 9 (Section 2).

[4]San Angelo *Standard,* October 9, 1886, p. 3. In August of 1887, Guillermo Alderette paid taxes on land evaluated at $6,480. Ibid., August 20, 1887, p. 3.

[5]Ibid., September 15, 1888, p. 7.

[6]Ibid., May 9, 1891, pp. 1, 3.

[7]Tom Green County Tax Rolls, 1890, 1895.

[8]Bill Green Papers.

[9]San Angelo *Standard,* February 3, 1906, p. 9.

[10]Tom Green County Tax Rolls, 1900.

[11]Bill Green Papers.

[12]San Angelo *Standard,* February 3, 1906, p. 9.

[13]Ibid., December 16, 1912, p. 1; December 17, 1913, p. 1.

José Ángel Alderette[1]

A pure-blooded Indian—some say from a tribe in Mexico—adopted by Pablo Alderette, José Ángel accompanied his foster father to the Concho Country in the years immediately after the founding of Fort Concho. A freighter during his younger days, he took an active interest in the affairs of the region, voted in Tom Green County's first election in 1876, and signed the petition to disincorporate San Angelo in 1904. During the latter part of his life, he acted as caretaker to Mrs. Kate Veck, his stepsister, helping her with a flower shop she had managed since San Angelo's early years. José Ángel Alderette died in 1930 at the age of 83.

[1]Sources for this sketch are the same ones used in structuring the life of the Alderette family. For José Ángel's connection to that family, see the Alderette genealogy table. A short biographical sketch on him is in San Angelo *Morning Standard,* February 4, 1930, p. 5.

Reynaldo Camúñez and Otilia Marquardt[1]

The Camúñez name surfaces regularly in the records of the early Concho Country. Reynaldo Camúñez Sr., and his wife, Otilia Marquardt Camúñez, for example, played important roles in early Hispanic activities and left a legacy for modern San Angelo.

Originally from New Mexico, Reynaldo Camúñez came to Santa Ángela sometime in the 1870s. Reynaldo found work at Bismarck Farm, where he raised vegetables for the soldiers at Fort Concho and met his future bride, Otilia Marquardt, a German from Fredericksburg who already was the mother of a little girl named Kate. After a brief courtship, Reynaldo and Otilia married in 1881.

From farm work, Don Reynaldo turned to freighting, eventually passing on his business to his sons Reynaldo Jr. and Frank. In the early twentieth century, the younger Reynaldo's wagons, mules, and horses moved across the Concho Country transporting lumber, wire, and food. Reportedly, it was Reynaldo Camúñez Jr. who brought one of the first oil rigs to West Texas.

Reynaldo's brother Frank's specialty was house-moving, though he later entered the mercantile business. In the 1930s, Frank served as one of the area's deputy sheriffs.

Numerous well-known contemporary San Angeleños trace their heritage to the marriage of Reynaldo and Otilia Marquardt Camúñez, with the children of the Reynaldo Jr. and Josefa Lara marriage among the most accomplished. Eva Camúñez set a precedent in 1930 as the first native San Angeloan of Hispanic descent to graduate from the city's high school. She later attended San Angelo Junior College, Sul Ross College, and the University of Texas, and became principal and teacher in the Ballinger Mexican School in the late 1930s and early 1940s. Today, she remains an avid supporter of San Angelo humanitarian causes and has contributed time, energy, and money to further church activities and educational programs.

Her brother, Noé Camúñez, now deceased, was San Angelo's first Mexican American school principal, serving at Sam Houston Elementary School from 1950-53. His greatest accomplishment, however, took place in San Antonio, where he established a reputation as an educational innovator from 1953 to 1976.

Helen Robles Martínez is another descendent of Reynaldo and Otilia Camúñez who left a mark in San Angelo. A graduate of San Angelo High School in 1935, she and her husband Frank managed a grocery store on South Chadbourne in the 1940s, helped Mexican Americans with their draft registration during World War II, and wrote letters to the city newspaper editor protesting the disparaging portrayal of Mexican Americans during the war decade. Mrs. Martinez continued active in civic matters in the 1950s and at the age of fifty received her college degree. Before her

[1]Eva Camúñez de Tucker interview, December 10, 1982; San Angelo *Morning Times,* May 9, 1934, p. 1; San Angelo *Standard-Times,* January 24, 1943, p. 5 (Section 1), August 19, 1966, p. 2A, February 23, 1969, p. 4B, September 24, 1972, p. 2A; and Tom Green County Censuses of 1880 and 1910; Helen Robles Martinez interview, May 22, 1984; Documents provided by Frank A. Martinez, copies in author's possession.

retirement in the latter 1970s, she served as a public school teacher.

George Jaimes, another San Angeleño descended from Reynaldo and Otilia Camúñez, joined LULAC in the late 1930s and continued his civic involvement until his death in the late 1970s. George was among San Angelo's first Mexican American policemen.

Antonio Flores and Marcelina Marrujo[1]

Antonio Flores came to San Angelo from Monclova, México, probably in the late 1870s. In the 1880s, he married Marcelina Marrujo, daughter of another of the city's early families. A painter by trade, he regularly worked under Oscar Ruffini, the famed early architect of the Concho Country, painting several of the latter's buildings.

Among the better known of Antonio and Marcelina's offspring is Nicolás Flores, 17 West 9th Street. At the age of ninety, Don Nicolás still has an incredibly vivid memory of early San Angelo and can be counted upon as a reliable source of information on Mexican Americans since the early years of the twentieth century.

Another well known descendant of Antonio and Marcelina Flores is their grandson Tony Flores. His tailor shop has been situated at the same location at 31A West Twohig Avenue for many years.

[1]Tom Green County censuses in 1900, and 1910; tax rolls, 1881; and interview with Nicolás Flores, October 20, 1982.

Félix Flores and Justa Herrera[1]

Félix Flores and Justa Herrera Flores came from San Antonio to Ben Ficklin in 1875. From there, the family moved to Knickerbocker, Texas, where they worked for the Tweedy brothers. They next moved to Sherwood, Texas, ultimately settling in San Angelo in 1884 on land south of the North Concho River. The tax rolls of 1885 show Félix Flores as owning property valued at $650.00 in the Millspaugh Addition.

The fate of Félix is unclear; he apparently died in the 1890s, for the Tom Green County census in 1900 lists Justa as head of a household of four boys. By then the men were on their own; Juan, the oldest, had appeared on Tom Green County tax rolls as early as 1878. In the 1890s, he was an active member in San Angelo's community life—having a role in a Mexican play presented in 1896 and attending the fiestas patrias celebrations during that decade. A man of acute business sense, he sold part of his land on South Irving Street to the Orient Railroad line for $5,000, supposedly for the company's headquarters and shop. In that period, he also operated a labor agency that supplied outlying ranches with farm hands.

Juan's marriage to Virginia Camúñez resulted in nine children, including the well-known Dan Flores. Like his father before him, Dan made his livelihood as a sheep shearer, though more in the capacity of a *capitán* (boss) than as a *tasinque* (shearer).

Of the four children born to Félix and Justa Flores, however, the one to contribute most to the city of San Angelo was José Flores Sr. He came to the Concho Country as an infant, grew up in San Angelo, then departed for Add Ran College in Hood County as a teenager in 1891. After working in El Paso, New Mexico, and Arizona as a labor agent, he returned to the Concho Country in 1899.

Copying his brother and uncle, he handled a labor agency from 1906 until the early 1930s. These years embraced one of the more productive phases of his life. In 1910, he took part in the school boycott; from the 1910s through the 1930s, he held a leadership role in the fiestas patrias; in 1928, when Sam Houston Elementary school opened its doors, he thrust himself into school activities; and in the early 1930s, he helped found LULAC Council 27.

About this time, he began losing his eyesight and thus commenced the second phase of his productive life—a long career as reporter and interpreter in the city courts. Probably the most famous case in which José Flores acted as an interpreter was the one involving Frank Salazar. On December 17, 1938, Salazar allegedly killed a white couple he worked for on a ranch in Runnels County and left the two daughters for dead. José Flores' job during the trial, which was held in Sweetwater in early 1939 and given wide newspaper coverage, was to search for Spanish-speaking witnesses, question them, and interpret for the court. The jury rendered a verdict of guilty and sentenced Salazar to be executed. Suspicions that Salazar had been wrongfully accused remained for years after the trial.

During World War II, José Flores carried out substantial work in behalf of the government. For these efforts, he was awarded the Selective Service Medal for volunteer work in 1946.

In the 1940s and 1950s, José Flores continued active, working out of his residence at 1701 South Chadbourne. He served as a liaison between Hispanics and attorneys and helped others during periods of difficulties.

[1]Tom Green County censuses in 1880, 1900, and 1910; interview with Herminia Flores, November 10, 1982, and Inez Tafolla, June 22, 1983; San Angelo *Standard,* September 9, 1909, p. 4; Fort Worth *Star-Telegram,* January 25, 1939; numerous stories on Frank Salazar case in San Angelo *Morning Standard,* starting December 18, 1938 and continuing until the latter part of 1939; San Angelo *Standard-Times,* May 25, 1964, p. 2; Tom Green County Tax Rolls, 1880, 1885, 1890, 1895, 1900; correspondence with Elida Robertson, April 30, 1984. Joe I. Flores, Jr., of Cleburne, Texas (great grandson of Félix Flores) contributed vital information on this Flores family. Correspondence dated April 28, 1984, in author's files.

Other descendants of Félix Flores and Justa Herrera family have played a part in San Angelo history. Among these was José P. (Chacho) Flores (son of José Flores Sr.), who was an amateur boxer of some standing in the 1930s and 1940s; winning the Texas light-heavyweight championship highlighted his twelve year career. He died on October 8, 1983, of a sudden illness.

Zoila Guerrero, wife of Máximo Guerrero, is another descendant of Félix and Justa Flores who still resides in San Angelo. Máximo was a civic leader in the Hispanic community from the 1920s through the 1960s. Zoila has served in city schools for years.

Anastacio Marrujo and Rosario Caravajal[1]

Anastacio Marrujo, a Cherokee Indian, came to San Angelo in the 1870s with his wife, Rosario Soto Caravajal. The 1880 census shows that the Marrujo family had several children and that Anastacio was working as a ranch hand. Señor Marrujo died at the age of 105.

The only son of this union apparently left for California in the 1920s or 1930s; several sisters followed him. Therefore, the Marrujo name, prominent in the early days, no longer exists in San Angelo. Descendants of the girls who stayed in the city may still reside here. Their names, however, necessarily changed through marriage.

[1]Nicolás Flores interview, October 20, 1982; Tom Green County censuses of 1880, 1900 and 1910. Tom Green County Tax Rolls, 1880, 1885, 1890, 1895.

Ignacio Morán and Luisa Chávez[1]

The Morán brothers—Florencio, Clemente, and Ignacio—came to the Concho Country from San Antonio sometime in the 1880s. Little is known of Clemente and Florencio, though the latter's name makes an appearance on the Tom Green County tax rolls by the late 1880s.

More information is available on Ignacio Morán and his part in local history. In the Concho Country, he met and married Lucía Chávez, an immigrant to the area from Las Limpias, a settlement in the Big Bend. Like other working people in the San Angelo area in its formative period, Ignacio found jobs on sheep ranches and did a variety of field work, including grubbing. In the latter tasks, the entire family accompanied him.

After a stay in Coleman from about 1909 to 1920, the family returned to San Angelo. The Morán name then became identifiable with different aspects of the fiestas patrias celebrations and other activities in town.

Among the descendants still living in San Angelo is eighty-six-year-old Cruz ("Cuche") Morán, a well-known yard-man and an accomplished amateur singer.

[1]Cruz Morán interview, September 23, 1982.

Florentino Muñoz[1]

Florentino Muñoz's name appears regularly in the San Angelo newspapers of the 1890s in connection with a variety of local affairs. A saloon keeper most of his time in the city, he was also a member of several fraternal clubs, including San Angelo's lodge of Obreros del Universo.

Muñoz led the school boycott of 1910. A committed civil rights advocate, he demanded equality for the Hispanic community during the heat of the controversy. In an eloquent moment, he stated:

> Under the system which now prevails, the Mexican children are learning nothing—they have never learned anything, and we are simply seeking our just rights. We have the right to put our children in the white schools and we are going to do it, if we have to go to the highest authorities in the state.
>
> No, we will not accept the proposition of the school board, which is to give us a school north of the railroad and south of the river. This is not satisfactory to us. We want to send them from the school districts in which they live to the schools of that district.

As head of the boycott committee, Muñoz sought the assistance of the Mexican consul in San Antonio and came to symbolize the solidarity of the Mexican American community against educational segregation.

Muñoz disappeared from San Angelo in the early 1920s—the 1921 city directory was the last to list him. His descendants moved out of town in the 1920s.

[1]Tom Green County censuses of 1900 and 1910; San Angelo *Standard,* September 11, 1909, p. 2; interview with Inez Tafolla, June 22, 1983; De León, "Blowout 1910 Style."

Jesús Tafolla and Prajedes Fuentes[1]

The Tafollas rank among that select group of families in today's San Angelo who trace their arrival in the Concho Country back to the 1870s (there is no connection to José Tafoya, the famed Indian guide of early Fort Concho). Originally from Piedras Negras,

México, the first glimpse one gets of the name is in 1880 when the census lists Jesús Tafolla as married to Prajedes Tafolla and heading a family of four children.

The early newspapers associate this family—especially three of the boys, Santos, Jesús Jr., and José—as active in Hispanic community affairs. Santos tried his hand at acting in the 1896 play, "In the Hilt of the Sword," for instance, and the three were fixtures at fiestas patrias observances in that era. The marriage of Jesús Jr. to Felipa Romo ranked as one of the important social events of the early twentieth century, for the San Angelo *Standard* devoted a full story to it and mentioned almost all the well-known "first families" of the city as joining in the celebration.

José Tafolla enjoyed a successful career as a restaurant owner while simultaneously running a labor agency on West Concho Avenue through the 1920s. It was in that area of town that José met a tragic death in 1925 in a gun battle with police. The causes for the fight are convoluted—Mexican Americans tell one story, Anglos another. What occurred is vividly etched, however, both in the report of the *Standard* and the stories perpetuated orally by eyewitnesses. On that fateful night of September 6, at 2:00 a.m., practically the entire police force collected a distance from a house at Irving Street near the river, then perforated Tafolla's refuge with gunfire as dozens of spectators watched. City hardware stores had been opened up to give officers access to ammunition and dynamite with which they attempted to blow up Tafolla's hideout.

José left an ambitious family. His son Inez helped organize the Alianza Hispano-Americana in 1928 and a few years later was instrumental in bringing LULAC to town—he served as vice president in 1931. Dora Tafolla, a daughter, also sought a role in social organizations; she was queen of the Emilio Carranza Lodge of the Spanish American Alliance in 1929. In the 1930s, other offspring of the José Tafolla family took to political affairs, Rudolf Tafolla endorsing Penrose Metcalfe for State Senator in 1938. Today, the younger generation remains active in the affairs of the city. Alex Tafolla ran unsuccessfully for the city council in 1977, was LULAC president in 1982-1983, and is the Community Development and Housing Director today.

Other branches of the Jesús and Prajedes Tafolla union also left a mark in San Angelo records. Henry and Beatrice Tafolla, the two children of Anastacio, were prominent members of the local LULAC chapter in the late 1930s and 1940s. This branch of the family, however, has long since left the city.

[1]Tom Green County censuses of 1880, 1900, 1910; Tom Green County Tax Rolls, 1880, 1885, 1890, 1895, 1900; San Angelo *Standard,* February 3, 1906, p. 3; September 6, 1925, p. 1; September 8, 1925, p. 3; San Angelo *Morning Times,* September 9, 1928, p. 9 (Section 1); May 12, 1929, p. 24-3 (Section 1); August 12, 1931, p. 7; July 17, 1928, p. 8 (Section 3); and Inez Tafolla interview, June 22, 1983.

Adolfo Varela and Damasia María Alderette[1]

A prominent stockman in early San Angelo, according to primary sources, Adolfo Varela in 1884 married Damasia María Alderette, daughter of Pablo and Ramona Alderette. As of 1890, he owned acreage worth $800.00, plus livestock and wagons valued at $460.00. His land was situated on the North Concho River next to property belonging to Guillermo Alderette.

Adolfo's interests included developing the cultural life of the city's Hispanic community. To this end, he served as president of the Sociedad Fraternal Unión México-Texana for a time, starting in 1897, and involved the organization in such events as fiestas patrias commemorations. Not much is known of his later years in the city, and the fate of his descendants—if any—is undetermined.

[1]San Angelo *Standard,* September 30, 1899, p. 1; San Angelo *Standard-Times,* May 3, 1934, p. 4 (Section 4); Marriage Records, Volume I, Tom Green County Courthouse; Tom Green County Tax Rolls, 1880, 1885, 1890, 1895.

Ramona (Wuertemburg) Alderette

Ramona Wuertemburg and her children—Catalina, Nestor, Charles, and Phillipi—were among the first Hispanic settlers of the Concho Country, coming to the area with the head of the household, Pablo Alderette. Ramona's first husband, a Union soldier from Fredericksburg named Philip J. Wuertemburg,[1] died in a Confederate prison camp in 1862.[2] Ramona and her four children by Wuertemburg became members of the Alderette family with the marriage of Ramona to Pablo in the 1860s. Pablo clearly assumed a parental role, and the children at times even used the last name of Alderette instead of Wuertemburg. Raised in a Mexican American atmosphere, all spoke Spanish and carried on Hispanic traditions as inculcated into them by their mother and stepfather.[3]

Catalina Wuertemburg became the most prominent of the four Wuertemburg children. At the age of fourteen, she married forty-four-year-old W. S. Veck, one of San Angelo's most distinguished businessmen and promoters in the period before 1900. For years, she was credited, albeit erroneously, with having suggested the name of "Santa Ángela" to Bart DeWitt as an appropriate name for the town DeWitt founded.[4] In the late nineteenth and early twentieth centuries she owned and operated a flower shop on Concho Avenue and is known as the town's "pioneer florist."[5]

Charles, Nestor, and Phillipi Wuertemburg also played conspicuous roles in the early affairs of the Concho Country. Charles voted in the first Tom Green County election in 1876 and was among those petitioning to disincorporate San Angelo in 1904.

In later years, he entered the house-moving business. He also was an accomplished musician and a dance empresario. His dance hall on Ninth Street was the scene of many a festive affair as late as the 1920s.

Nestor entered the freighting business soon after his arrival in the Concho Country, earning his livelihood by selling wood and hay to the fort. One of his sons, José, was among the city's first Mexican American policeman,[6] and a grandson, Nestor III (son of Nestor II), pursued the same career.

Phillipi Wuertemburg, the youngest sibling, also took an interest in local affairs, petitioning with his brother Charles for the disincorporation of San Angelo in 1904. According to a biographical sketch written by members of the West Texas Museum in the 1930s, he was successful in real estate and claimed valuable holdings in the form of duplexes and apartments as late as the Depression years.[7] In the mid-1930s, he disappeared from the San Angelo scene.

[1]According to a story that has come down through the years (first told by Phillipi), the original family name was "Walschenburg" (or something akin to that). The family did not like it, so they changed it to Wuertemburg. One of the descendants, Nestor Wuertenburg III, says that the U.S. Army changed his name to Wuertenburg during World War II, that he kept the spelling after that, and other family members retained the new designation. Bill Green Papers; Nestor Wuertenburg III interview, July 12, 1983.

[2]San Angelo *Standard,* June 20, 1924, p. 5.

[3]Estrada family interview; Cruz Morán interview; Nestor Wuertenburg III interview, Lola Wuertenburg interview, July 16, 1983.

[4]San Angelo *Standard,* October 25, 1916, p. 6, May 3, 1924, p. 3 (Section 2); San Angelo *Morning Times,* April 7, 1936, p. 12; Daniel, "San Angelo Receives a New Name."

[5]San Angelo *Morning Times,* September 17, 1933, p. 2 (Section 1); April 7, 1936, p. 12.

[6]San Angelo *Morning Times,* June 20, 1929, p. 1; June 21, 1929, p. 13; September 7, 1930, p. 3.

[7]Ibid., June 20, 1929, p. 1 (Section 1); May 3, 1934, p. 4 (Section 4); "Sketches of the Early Settlers of the Concho Country" (West Texas Museum, 1933), typescript at Barker Texas History Center, University of Texas Archives, Austin, pp. 130-147.

What Ever Happened to the Alderettes and the Wuertemburgs?

Pablo Alderette and Ramona Silva Wuertemburg Alderette arrived in the Concho Country in 1869 or 1870. Their names would become etched in the lore of the region for years thereafter.

Several Mexican American families came about the same time as Pablo and Ramona and made significant contributions to San Angelo history, but unique circumstances set the Alderette/Wuertemburg names apart. Pablo Alderette, for example, was one of the first commissioners to serve Tom Green County. He wielded political power throughout the 1870s and was one of the wealthiest men in the Concho Country during that time. His son Guillermo, a child from his first marriage, also played significant political roles in the 1870s and was highly regarded as a farmer and a stockman up to the 1880s.

Then, Catalina (Kate) Wuertemburg, stepdaughter of Pablo and biological offspring of Ramona and her first husband Philip, married the prominent businessman W. S. Veck in 1872. Her marriage to a man who played such a critical role in the early growth of San Angelo would have permanently inscribed the Wuertemburg name in the records, but further, the union was seen as near scandalous in that period: it was a mixed marriage, and Veck was a whiskey seller, a Protestant, and thirty years the fourteen-year-old girl's senior. Kate also held an important position in local history by mistake. Until 1946, historians erroneously credited Kate with suggesting that the town be named "Santa Ángela."

Why Pablo and Ramona Alderette were motivated to come to the Concho Country is unclear and, indeed, very little is known about their respective backgrounds. From what can be pieced together, it appears that Pablo Alderette was born in New Mexico in the late 1810s—the Tom Green County census of 1880 shows him to be 63 years old. From his first wife Susana (last name unknown), he had one child, the aforementioned Guillermo. During the Civil War, Pablo remarried in San Antonio, Texas. His new wife, Ramona Silva Wuertemburg, originally came from New Mexico. She was the widow of a soldier named Philip J. Wuertemburg, who died a prisoner of war in a Confederate prison camp in 1862 at Camp Verde, Texas. Ramona and Philip produced four children—Catalina (the wife of W. S. Veck), Charles, Nestor, and Phillipi Wuertemburg.

When the couple headed for West Texas and a new beginning, the family included the children by their first marriages, plus two girls of their own—Severa and Jesusita—and José Ángel Alderette, an Indian from Mexico adopted by Pablo. Another girl, Damasia María, probably the twin sister of Severa, was left in the care of *padrinos* (godparents) in Laredo, according to one source, but was reunited with the Alderettes in the 1870s. The family settled along the North Concho River on sections of land which later became part of the Pulliam Ranch. In the Concho Country, Doña Ramona bore five more children: Grivaldo, Pantaleón, Antonio, Alberto, and Clara.

Three different branches of the same family, then, took root in the early Concho Country and passed on the Alderette and Wuertemburg names. Though all grew up in an Hispanic ambience and most had Spanish first names, some of them became anglicized to the degree that they lost their cultural connection to Pablo and Ramona. Others retained their *mexicanidad* ("Mexicanness") in its entirety, to the point that they carried on Mexican culture with a German name like Wuertemburg.

Of the children born to Pablo and Ramona, Jesusita (Susie) married James B. Keating, a prominent member of early Anglo American society and the Tom Green county clerk from 1908 to 1935. The Keating children received strong dosages of Mexican American culture from Jesusita but married Anglo Americans. Clara Alderette, another child of Pablo and Ramona, reportedly married several times but may not have raised a family. The same may have been the case with Damasia Alderette Varela. Severa Alderette Gómez married, and some of her descendants now live in Big Spring, Texas. The four boys—Grivaldo, Pantaleón, Antonio, and Alberto—apparently produced no children. Indeed, only Alberto survived his mother (who died in 1924), and that only by one year. If, in fact, the men never reproduced, this branch of the Alderette family did not perpetuate the name.

Guillermo Alderette, Pablo's son by his first marriage, on the other hand, fathered seven offspring. He married Ricarda Delgado, reportedly in the Concho Country, and the couple taught their family Mexican American ways.

Their first son, William Alderette II, married Oliva Addicks. Although he died young—as the result of a fall from a horse in 1898—he left two children, Guillermo III and Ricarda. The son seemingly left for San Antonio and never returned to San Angelo. The other child, Ricarda, vanished into obscurity.

Antonio Alderette, the second son of Guillermo and Ricarda, met his death in 1906 at the Gray Mule Saloon on Concho Avenue. He left no heirs.

Pablo Alderette, the third son, married Isabel Samarrón, descendant of one of the early families in the city and left one daughter—Pauline Alderette—at the time of his death in 1912. Pauline married twice. She produced three children by her first husband (the children left for California in the 1950s) and six by her second husband, the late Gumesindo García. The García progeny reside in San Angelo today, among them Dolores Garcia, who is the wife of the author of this book.

Ajeo Alderette, the last son of the elder Guillermo, was killed one year after his brother Pablo. He left no children from his marriage to Maria Lara.

Marcelina Alderette, one of the daughters of Don Guillermo and Doña Ricarda Alderette, married Senón Estrada. They raised ten children, most of whom departed for California long ago. John Estrada is the only member of this union remaining in San Angelo; he resides with his family at 1802 North Magdalen.

Micaela Alderette, another daughter of Guillermo and Ricarda, married José Tafolla, son of one of the early Hispanic settlers in San Angelo; the couple reared sixteen children. The children became active participants in the affairs of the town, and by the 1920s held memberships in numerous organizations intended to better conditions for Mexican Americans. In the 1930s, the names of Dora Tafolla and Inez Tafolla were closely identified with fiestas patrias celebrations and LULAC efforts. Over the years, the family scattered to other parts of the country, primarily California, but those who remained have stayed active in civic matters. Alex Tafolla currently serves as Community Development and Housing Director for the City.

Aurelia Alderette, the last child of Guillermo and Ricarda Alderette, had three children, but little can be determined about the present status of this family. When last heard from, they were living in Oklahoma.

In the end, the Alderette name in San Angelo perished because the Alderette men produced only one boy, and he seemingly left town at an early age. Present-day families by the same name are not related to the Pablo Alderette of the 1870s. The Alderette daughters, on the other hand, maintained the family and its Mexican American culture in San Angelo. All of Guillermo and Ricarda Alderette's children and grandchildren grew up in predominantly Mexican American neighborhoods in San Angelo. More recent generations, however, have grown up in bicultural settings, and the majority of the young generation—born in the 1960s—use English as a first language and live in households where Mexican and Anglo cultures coexist.

Ramona Wuertemburg's children by Philip J. Wuertemburg were also reared as Mexican Americans and spoke the Spanish language well. But they took different ethnic paths—two intermarried with whites and assimilated themselves into Anglo society; the other two retained their allegiance to Mexican culture and raised their families accordingly.

The most prominent of Ramona's offspring turned out to be Catalina Wuertemburg Veck, whose importance has already been noted. The Vecks produced ten children, many of whom left San

Angelo in the early twentieth century. All seemingly became Anglo Americans; those paying their last respects upon her death in 1936 were almost entirely Anglo Americans.

The youngest son, Phillipi, followed the same course as his sister. He married Caroline Iffland, who gave him four sons, then married Lula M. Freelander upon Caroline's death. As of the 1930s, two of his sons lived in California, one in Colorado, and the other resided in another part of Texas.

In contradistinction to Kate and Phillipi, Charles Wuertemburg raised the family he produced with Trinidad Galván in Mexican American environs. Little can be determined of his descendants; practically none are left in the city. Carlos reportedly was killed when he fell from a tree into the North Concho River in 1905, and Santiago apparently left the city in the 1920s or 1930s. Elicio took an Anglo woman as his second wife; it has been impossible to locate any of their children. The fourth son, Marcos, had only daughters, gave them anglicized names, and never returned to San Angelo. He died in Ohio in 1976. Luisa, the only daughter of Charles and Trinidad, married three times, each time to a Mexican American, and the family she produced with Joseph Anaya now resides in Leavenworth, Kansas.

Nestor Wuertemburg, a fourth issue of Ramona and Philip J. Wuertemburg, married Pánfila Carreón, and they reared their children as Mexican Americans. Many of Nestor and Pánfila's descendants reside in San Angelo today, and the name of Wuertemburg (now spelled as Wuertenburg), preserved through this line, is well known within the Hispanic community.

Of the eight progeny born to Nestor and Pánfila Wuertemburg, José married Emilia Camúñez, scion of one of earliest families in San Angelo. Though a teamster for a good part of his life, José entered police work in the 1920s, serving as one of San Angelo's first Mexican American peace officers into the 1930s. His children still live, among them Carmen Vélez, wife of Henry V. Vélez, the activist civic leader from the 1940s up to the present.

Jesús, the second son of Nestor and Pánfila, had no family by his marriage to Felicita Garza. Two other sons, Felipe and Refugio, never married.

Another son, Nestor II, died at the age of seventy, leaving eight children. One of his sons, Nestor III, pursued a career in law enforcement and in 1981 retired after thirty-two years on the police forces of Tom Green County and San Angelo.

Maria, a sixth child of Nestor and Pánfila, married Frank Camúñez, brother of the aforementioned Emilia (wife of José Wuertemburg), and had six children. Part of this family maintains roots in San Angelo; some of the members, however, have dispersed to other regions in Texas and to California.

Flora Wuertemburg had seven children from the marriage to

SAN ANGELEÑOS

Nicolás García. Some family members make San Angelo their home today.

The youngest child of Nestor and Pánfila, Ramona Wuertemburg Muela, lives at 225 West Avenue M. Her only daughter, Soledad, married Elías Menchaca, and this family of ten is very much part of the San Angeleño culture.

So, what did happen to the Alderettes and the Wuertemburgs? First, part of the biological family of Pablo and Ramona Alderette became anglicized, and some of the descendants probably make their home in San Angelo under Anglo American names. The descendants of the girls who married Mexican Americans live elsewhere. The boys had no known children; thus the Alderette name has not survived through this line.

Second, the descendents of Pablo Alderette and his first wife invariably remained true to their Mexican heritage. Many of them reside in San Angelo, still as Mexican Americans. All, however, go by a name other than Alderette, because the sons of Guillermo the elder left no known male offspring.

Lastly, of the descendants of Ramona Silva Wuertemburg and Philip J. Wuertemburg, the most visible in today's San Angelo are the offspring of Nestor I—others go by another name, and many have left the city. The Wuertemburg name is not a common one and is perpetuated only by the few male grandchildren of the elder Nestor. As is the case with the Alderette descendants, the rest trace their link to Ramona Wuertemburg (the early settler) solely through the female ties.

NOTES

This story of the Alderettes and Wuertemburgs is based upon: Clemens, *The Concho Country;* Bill Green Papers; Tom Green County Censuses in 1880, 1900, and 1910; Marriage Records deposited at Tom Green County Courthouse; San Angelo City Directories; genealogy of W. S. Veck in author's possession, courtesy of Katharine Waring; letter from Joy Anaya, a descendant of the Wuertemburgs, dated April 15, 1983; interviews with Cruz Morán, Eva Camúñez de Tucker, Inez Tafolla, Otilia Camúñez Cerda, Ramona Wuertenburg Muela, Nestor Wuertenburg III, Lola Wuertemburg, Nicolás Flores, Estrada family, and María Estrada, July 29, 1983; San Angelo *Standard,* September 15, 1888, p. 7, February 25, 1905, p. 5, August 20, 1917, p. 1, October 15, 1916, p. 6, July 14, 1922, p. 1, May 3, 1924, p. 3 (Section 2), June 20, 1924, p. 5, May 4, 1925, p. 1, September 6, 1925, p. 1; San Angelo *Morning Standard,* September 9, 1928, p. 9, June 20, 1929, p. 1 (Section 1), February 4, 1930, p. 5, May 3, 1934, p. 4 (Section 4), April 7, 1936, p. 12; San Angelo *Standard-Times,* March 31, 1958, p. 2; and "Sketches of the Early Settlers of the Concho Country," pp. 130-147.

Family Trees

Alderette I

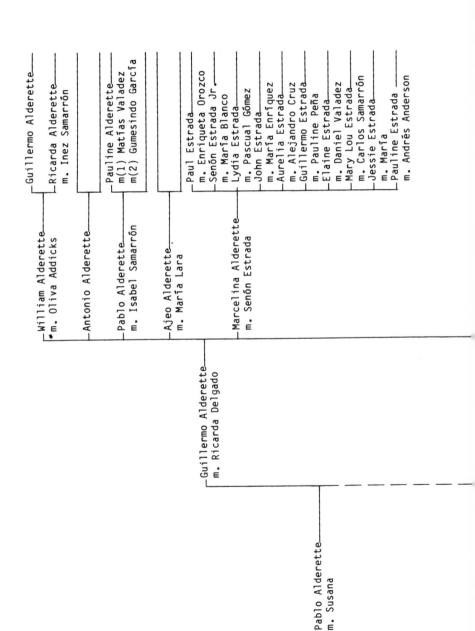

Guillermo Alderette
m. Ricarda Delgado

Guillermo Alderette

Ricarda Alderette
m. Inez Samarrón

William Alderette
m. Oliva Addicks

Antonio Alderette

Pauline Alderette
m(1) Matías Valadez
m(2) Gumesindo García

Pablo Alderette
m. Isabel Samarrón

Ajeo Alderette
m. María Lara

Marcelina Alderette
m. Senón Estrada

Paul Estrada
m. Enriqueta Orozco
Senón Estrada Jr.
m. María Blanco
Lydia Estrada
m. Pascual Gómez
John Estrada
m. María Enríquez
Aurelia Estrada
m. Alejandro Cruz
Guillermo Estrada
m. Pauline Peña
Elaine Estrada
m. Daniel Valadez
Mary Lou Estrada
m. Carlos Samarrón
Jessie Estrada
m. María
Pauline Estrada
m. Andrés Anderson

Pablo Alderette
m. Susana

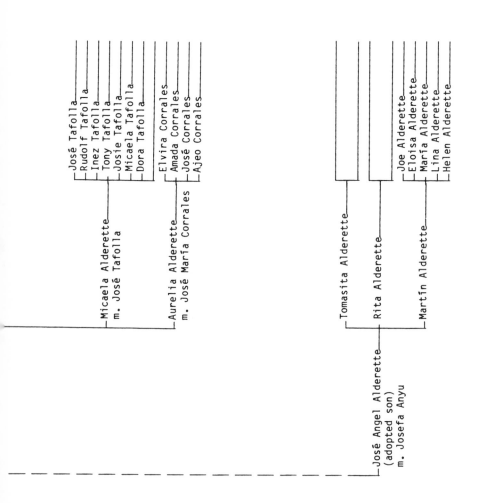

Alderette II

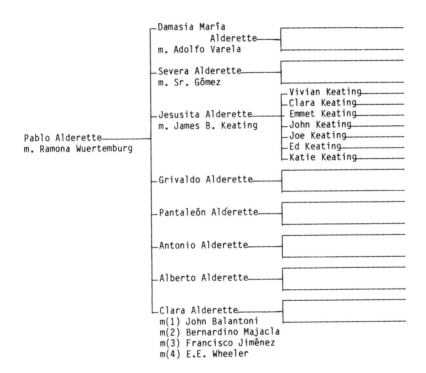

Pablo Alderette
m. Ramona Wuertemburg

- Damasia María
  Alderette
  m. Adolfo Varela

- Severa Alderette
  m. Sr. Gómez

- Jesusita Alderette
  m. James B. Keating
  - Vivian Keating
  - Clara Keating
  - Emmet Keating
  - John Keating
  - Joe Keating
  - Ed Keating
  - Katie Keating

- Grivaldo Alderette

- Pantaleón Alderette

- Antonio Alderette

- Alberto Alderette

- Clara Alderette
  m(1) John Balantoni
  m(2) Bernardino Majacla
  m(3) Francisco Jiménez
  m(4) E.E. Wheeler

Camúñez

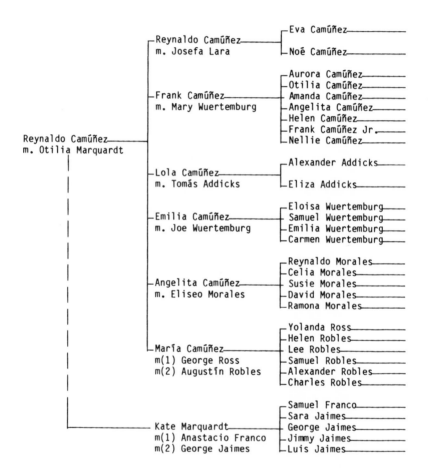

```
                                            ┌─Eva Camúñez─────────
                           ┌─Reynaldo Camúñez─┤
                           │ m. Josefa Lara    └─Noé Camúñez─────────
                           │
                           │                    ┌─Aurora Camúñez───────
                           │                    ├─Otilia Camúñez───────
                           │ ┌─Frank Camúñez─── ├─Amanda Camúñez───────
                           │ │ m. Mary Wuertemburg─┤─Angelita Camúñez──────
                           │ │                  ├─Helen Camúñez────────
                           │ │                  ├─Frank Camúñez Jr.─────
  Reynaldo Camúñez─────────┤ │                  └─Nellie Camúñez───────
  m. Otilia Marquardt      │ │
     │                     │ │                    ┌─Alexander Addicks──────
     │                     │ ├─Lola Camúñez──────┤
     │                     │ │ m. Tomás Addicks   └─Eliza Addicks───────
     │                     │ │
     │                     │ │                    ┌─Eloisa Wuertemburg────
     │                     │ ├─Emilia Camúñez──── ├─Samuel Wuertemburg────
     │                     │ │ m. Joe Wuertemburg ├─Emilia Wuertemburg────
     │                     │ │                    └─Carmen Wuertemburg────
     │                     │ │
     │                     │ │                    ┌─Reynaldo Morales──────
     │                     │ │                    ├─Celia Morales─────────
     │                     │ ├─Angelita Camúñez── ├─Susie Morales─────────
     │                     │ │ m. Eliseo Morales  ├─David Morales─────────
     │                     │ │                    └─Ramona Morales────────
     │                     │ │
     │                     │ │                    ┌─Yolanda Ross──────────
     │                     │ │                    ├─Helen Robles──────────
     │                     │ ├─María Camúñez───── ├─Lee Robles────────────
     │                     │ │ m(1) George Ross   ├─Samuel Robles─────────
     │                     │ │ m(2) Augustín Robles├─Alexander Robles──────
     │                     │ │                    └─Charles Robles────────
     │                     │ │
     │                     │ │                    ┌─Samuel Franco─────────
     │                     │ │                    ├─Sara Jaimes───────────
     └─────────────────────┘ └─Kate Marquardt─── ├─George Jaimes─────────
                               m(1) Anastacio Franco├─Jimmy Jaimes─────────
                               m(2) George Jaimes  └─Luis Jaimes───────────
```

Antonio Flores

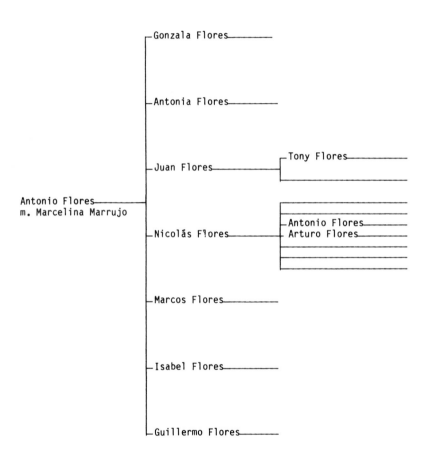

Félix Flores

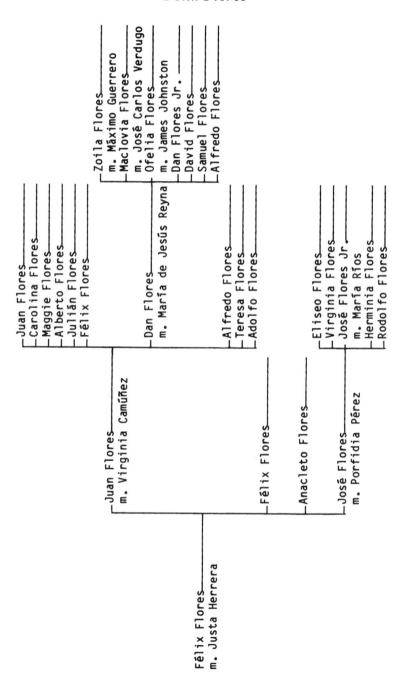

Tafolla

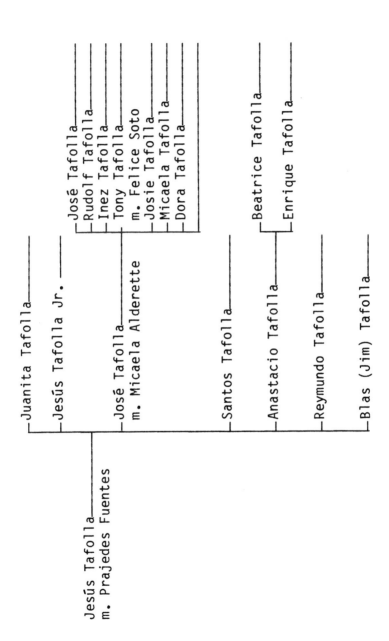

José Tafolla
Rudolf Tafolla
Inez Tafolla
Tony Tafolla
m. Felice Soto
Josie Tafolla
Micaela Tafolla
Dora Tafolla

Juanita Tafolla
Jesús Tafolla Jr.

José Tafolla
m. Micaela Alderette

Santos Tafolla

Anastacio Tafolla

Reymundo Tafolla

Blas (Jim) Tafolla

Beatrice Tafolla
Enrique Tafolla

Jesús Tafolla
m. Prajedes Fuentes

Varela

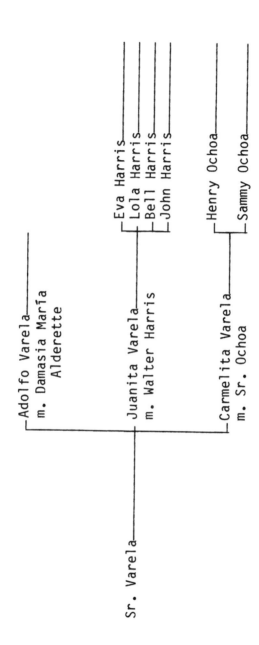

Wuertemburg

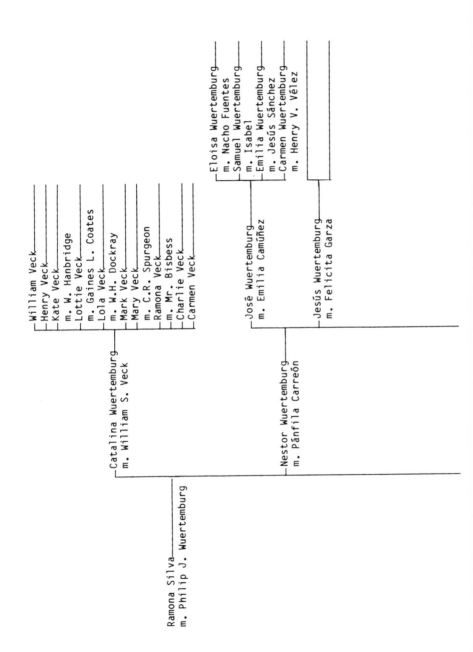

Nestor Wuertemburg II
m. Dolores Otero

- Nestor Wuertemburg III
  m. Isabel Domínguez
- Ofelia Wuertemburg
- George Jaimes
  m. George Jaimes
- Clorinda Wuertemburg
  m. José Muñoz
- Ernestine Wuertemburg
  m. Ralph González
- Viviana Wuertemburg
  m(1) Raymond Nava
  m(2) Matías Valadez
- Betty Wuertemburg
  m. Ausencio Alonzo
- Richard Wuertemburg
  m. Mary García
- Jimmy Wuertemburg

Refugio Wuertemburg

Felipe Wuertemburg

María Wuertemburg
m. Frank Camúñez

- Aurora Camúñez
  m. Enrique Johnson
- Amanda Camúñez
  m. Esequiel Rodríguez
- Angelita Camúñez
  m. Claude García
- Nellie Camúñez
  m. Sr. Ybarra
- Otilia Camúñez
- Frank Camúñez
  m. Elvira Gómez

- **Charles Wuertemburg** m. Trinidad Galván
  - **Flora Wuertemburg** m. Nicolás García
    - Nick García
    - Herminia García
    - Rodolfo García
    - Joe García
    - Santana García
    - Jessie Manuel García
    - María García
  - **Ramona Wuertemburg** m. Reyes Muela
    - Soledad Muela m. Elías Menchaca
  - **Carlos Wuertemburg**
  - **Santiago Wuertemburg** m. Jesusita Estrada
    - Carlos Wuertemburg
    - Santiago Wuertemburg
    - Sammy Wuertemburg
    - Trini Wuertemburg
    - Mary Lou Wuertemburg
  - **Elicio Wuertemburg** m. Alberta
    - Elaine Wuertemburg
  - **Luisa Wuertemburg** m(1) Pedro Zúñiga / m(2) Sr. de la Cruz / m(3) m. Joseph Anaya
    - Mildred Wuertemburg
    - Irene Zúñiga
    - Ernesto Zúñiga
    - Ofelia Zúñiga
    - Lupe de la Cruz
    - Frank Anaya
    - Joseph Anaya
    - Lois Anaya
    - Philip Anaya
  - **Marcos Wuertemburg** m(1) Flores Cortez / m(2) Clementine Tocci
    - Marklyn Wuertemburg
    - Mignon Wuertemburg

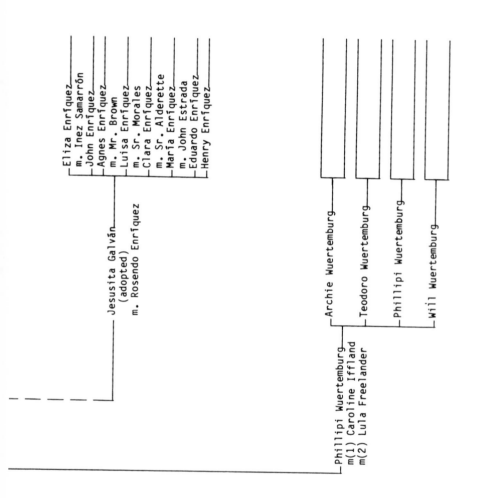

Bibliography

Manuscripts

"Sketches of the Early Settlers of the Concho Country." Typescript, West Texas Museum, 1933. Eugene C. Barker Texas History Center, University of Texas, Austin.

Census Records

Census of Tom Green County, 1880, 1900, 1910.

Eighteenth Census of the United States, *Census of Population: 1960,* Vol. I, Part A. Washington D.C.: Government Printing Office, 1961.

Fifteenth Census of the United States: 1930, *Population,* Vol. II. Washington D.C.: Government Printing Office, 1933.

Sixteenth Census of the United States, *Population,* Vol. I. Washington D.C.: Government Printing Office, 1942.

City Records of San Angelo

City Commission Minutes, Vol. 18, City Secretary's Office, City Hall, San Angelo, Texas.

San Angelo Comprehensive Plan, Part I. San Angelo: Department of Planning, 1977.

County Records of Tom Green County

Marriage Records, Vol. I, Tom Green County Courthouse.

Tom Green County Commissioners' Court Minutes, Volume A.

Tom Green County Tax Rolls, 1878 through 1900.

Newspapers

El Paso Times, El Paso, Texas, 1886.

Fort Worth *Star-Telegram,* Fort Worth, Texas, 1939.

Los Tiempos, San Angelo, Texas, 1983-1984.

San Angelo Magazine, San Angelo, Texas, February, 1983.

San Angelo *Standard-Times,* San Angelo, Texas, 1884-1984.

San Antonio *Express,* San Antonio, Texas, 1972.

West Texas Angelus, San Angelo, Texas, 1984.

Interviews

Eva Camúñez de Tucker, December 10, 1982, and April 4, 1983.
Otilia Camúñez Cerda, January 4, 1983.
Pete Chapa, May 23, 1984.
Gus Clemens, November 24, 1982.

SAN ANGELEÑOS

John Estrada family, October 27, 1982.
Herminia Flores, November 10, 1982.
Nicolás Flores, October 20, 1982.
Oscar C. Gómez, February 25, 1984.
Bill Green, November 17, 1982.
Máximo Guerrero, June 22, 1984.
Raymond Holguín, January 9, 1984.
Helen Robles Martínez, May 22, 1984.
Cruz Morán, September 23, 1982.
Ramona Wuertenberg Muela, November 10, 1982.
Inez Tafolla, June 22, 1983.
Henry V. Vélez, May 22, 1984.
Lola Wuertenburg, July 16, 1983.
Nestor Wuertenburg III, July 12, 1983.

Personal Papers

Bill Green Papers
Frank A. Martínez Papers

Correspondence

Joy Anaya letter, April 15, 1983.
Cato Cedillo letter, May 23, 1984.
Mario J. Cruz letter, February 27, 1984.
Joe I. Flores Jr. letter, April 28, 1984.
Aurora García letter, May 2, 1984.
Ed Idar Jr. letters, March 28, 1984, June 19, 1984.
Elida Robertson letter, April 30, 1984.

Books

Allsup, Carl. *The American G.I. Forum.* Center for Mexican American Studies, Monograph 6. Austin: University of Texas Press, 1982.

Carter, Robert. *On the Border with MacKenzie: or Winning West Texas from the Comanches.* Washington, D.C.: Eynon Printing Co., 1935.

Chávez, Tomás Jr. *Texas Mexican Presbyterians.* Midland, Texas: First Presbyterian Church Press, 1980.

Clemens, Gus. *The Concho Country.* San Antonio: Mulberry Avenue Books, 1980.

De León, Arnoldo. *Las Fiestas Patrias: Biographic Notes on the Hispanic Presence in San Angelo, Texas.* San Antonio: Caravel Press, 1978.

———*The Tejano Community, 1836-1900.* Albuquerque: University of New Mexico Press, 1982.

Green, Bill. *The Dancing was Lively: Fort Concho, Texas, A Social History 1867-1882.* San Angelo: Fort Concho Sketches Publishing Co., 1974.

Hodges, B. A. *A History of the Mexican Mission Work Conducted by the Presbyterian Church in the United States of America in the Synod of Texas,* Waxahachie: The Woman's Synodical of Texas, 1931, in Carlos E. Cortes, *Church Views of the Mexican American,* New York: Arno Press, 1974.

Perales, Alonso. *Are We Good Neighbors?* San Antonio: Artes Gráficas, 1948.

Bibliography

Quintanilla, Guadalupe C. and James B. Silman. *El Espiritu Siempre Eterno del México Americano.* Washington, D.C.: University Press of America, 1977.

Taylor, Nathaniel. *The Coming Empire, or Two Thousand Miles in Texas on Horseback.* Houston: N. T. Carlisle, 1936.

Vigil, James Diego. *From Indians to Chicanos: A Socio-cultural History.* St. Louis: C. V. Mosley, 1980.

Worley, John. *Worley's Directory of San Angelo.* Dallas: John Worley Directory Company, 1909-1939.

Articles

De León, Arnoldo. "Blowout 1910 Style: A Chicano School Boycott in West Texas." *Texana,* XII (1974), 124-140.

—— "*Los Tasinques* and the Sheepshearers' Union of North America: A Strike in West Texas, 1934." *West Texas Historical Association Yearbook,* LV (1979), 1-16.

—— "St. Joseph's Church: A History," *St. Joseph Church Memorial Dedication Book,* San Angelo, 1983.

Duke, Escal F. "A Population Study of Tom Green County." *West Texas Historical Association Yearbook,* LII (1976) 49-60.

Limón, José. "The Folk Performance of 'Chicano' and the Cultural Limits of Political Ideology," in Richard Bauman and Roger D. Abrahams, eds. "*And Other Neighborly Names": Social Process and Cultural Image in Texas Folklore.* Austin: University of Texas Press, 1981.

Theses and Dissertations

Bitner, Grace. "The History of Tom Green County, Texas." Master of Arts thesis, University of Texas, 1931.

McKay, Reynolds. "Texas Mexican Repatriation During the Great Depression." Ph.D. dissertation, University of Oklahoma, 1982.

Melton, Greg. "Trials by Nature: The Harsh Environment of Fort Concho, Texas." Master of Arts thesis, Abilene Christian University, 1981.

Index

81150086